ASSURING QUALITY IN HEALTH PROMOTION

How to develop standards of good practice

David Evans

Research Fellow
Institute for Health Policy Studies
University of Southampton

Michael J. Head

Formerly Health Promotion Manager
Dorset Health Commission

Viv Speller

Director of Health Promotion
Wessex Institute of Public Health Medicine
University of Southampton

WESSEX
INSTITUTE OF
PUBLIC
HEALTH
MEDICINE

A Wessex Institute of Public Health Medicine project in collaboration with the
Health Education Authority

Published by the Health Education Authority

ISBN 0 7521 0207 9 Standard edition ✓
ISBN 0 7521 0245 1 Standard edition with computer disc

© Health Education Authority 1994
First published 1994

Health Education Authority
Hamilton House
Mabledon Place
London WC1H 9TX

Typeset by BookEns Ltd, Baldock, Herts.
Printed in England by Cromwell Printers, Wiltshire.

CONTENTS

FOREWORD

Quality assurance is a key aspect of the development of any service within the NHS today.

The quality assurance movement is linked to the development of clinical audit and has evolved to the extent that it is now an integral part of the day to day work of health professionals.

However, this appreciation of the need for quality assurance is not matched by the availability of methods to measure it. This is especially true of those areas of health where success is achieved mainly in the long term and where some outcomes like attitudinal changes tend to be intangible.

This manual provides a practical answer to this dilemma. It brings together several methods and practical considerations for establishing, implementing and measuring quality assurance in health promotion. The result of extensive consultation, discussion and debate with practising health promoters, it is designed to be a tool for actual use by health professionals to assist in devising the best instruments for measuring quality in their work.

The statements and guidelines which are highlighted in each chapter, therefore reflect generally held views about the elements that create excellence in the practice of health promotion. Additionally, guidelines are illustrated by case studies drawn from local health promotion departments.

Feedback obtained during the pilot stages of this pack has clearly indicated that it has a role to play as a means of devising proper quality assurance. We accept that this is not an easy field of work to develop, certainly not without a great deal of trial and error. It is hoped that of the many efforts to develop work in this area, this pack will find a niche and will play its part in increasing ability and confidence in demonstrating ever-increasing success in the practice of health promotion. This is a goal well worth striving for.

We commend this pack to anyone who wants to improve the practice of health promotion.

Professor John Gabbay
Director, Wessex Institute of Public Health Medicine

Dr Spencer Hagard
Chief Executive, Health Education Authority

ACKNOWLEDGEMENTS

This pack would not have been possible without the support and contribution of a large number of health promotion specialists and others who have participated in the consultative process. We particularly would like to thank the members of the Project Management Committee: Russell Caplan, Pat Christmas, Professor John Gabbay and Elizabeth Lowe. Their ideas and constructive criticism were crucial to the development of the project. We would also like to acknowledge the important role played by the Health Education Authority's Strategic Advisory Group which originally developed the proposal for the project, and the international contribution made by Hans Saan of the Dutch Centre for Health Promotion and Health Education.

Our thanks as well to the many health promotion specialists, particularly in Wessex, who have commented on or discussed aspects of this pack, or who have participated in our seminars and workshops. Particular thanks to Mary Amos, Mike Brewin, Chris Chappell, Peter Duncan, Linda Ewles, Louise Finnis, Jeff French, Clare Griffin, Alison Learmonth, Ursula Miles, Brian Neeson, Tricia Parsons, Graham Rogers, Liz Rolls, Diane Scorer, Ina Simnett and Pat Vinycombe, and to Annette Hobbs and Jane Weeks for their excellent secretarial support. Needless to say, we take full responsibility for all errors and failings in the pack.

The publishers are grateful for permission to reproduce the following copyright material:

Figure 2.3 from L. Ewles and I. Simnett *Promoting health – a practical guide* (Scutari Press, 2nd edn, 1992)
Figure 5.1 from Zaltman and Duncan in R. Ellis and D. Whittington *Quality assurance in health care – a handbook* (Edward Arnold, 1993).

1 INTRODUCTION

'Quality assurance need not be intimidating or difficult ... It can even be fun!'

Summary

This chapter considers the rationale for quality assurance in health promotion and the need for this pack. After reading this chapter you should understand:

1. The reasons for developing quality assurance in health promotion.

2. The aims and the format of this pack.

This pack provides an easy-to-use manual for health promotion practitioners to assist them in developing their quality assurance strategies and programmes. It is intended to be equally useful to health promotion providers who wish to integrate a quality assurance approach into their existing work, and to purchasers who wish to commission quality services. We have tried to keep the materials as simple and as jargon-free as possible. The pack is not intended to be in any way prescriptive; it offers an approach to quality assurance which health promotion practitioners may wish to adapt and develop to meet their local needs. Quality assurance need not be intimidating or difficult; should build on current good practice and will lead to more effective work and greater job satisfaction. It can even be fun!

Aims of this pack

Many practitioners working in specialist health promotion services provide a quality service. Most, however, are only beginning to develop explicit quality assurance programmes and are not in a position to quantify the quality of their service, or to identify the areas in which they need to improve quality. With the increasing pressure for health promotion specialists to demonstrate the value of their work to purchasers, colleagues, users, the public, the government and themselves, there is a need to provide a recognised method for assessing quality. What is needed, is a relatively easy, efficient and inexpensive way of assessing quality in health promotion work more systematically.

The aims of this pack are:

- to provide health promotion practitioners with a theoretical framework within which to address quality assurance in their practice

- to offer a practical model of a quality assurance framework for practitioners

- to offer model standards and criteria which practitioners may use in their quality assurance programmes, and which may help them to identify other standards

1

- to identify the implications of quality assurance for purchasers and providers of health promotion services

- to help overcome some of the difficulties faced by practitioners in developing quality assurance.

How to use this pack

These materials can be used in a variety of ways by different health promotion practitioners. In developing this quality assurance framework we recognise that there are many different philosophies of health promotion, that practitioners use different approaches and that health promotion services are organised in different ways. The approach to quality we are advocating here may, however, be applied within a range of diverse services and organisations.

The materials are designed to be as flexible and user-friendly as possible. Each chapter begins with a summary and concludes with key points for easy reference. There are a number of individual or group exercises throughout the text. There are also several case studies with contact names to enable readers to network with other practitioners who have begun to develop quality assurance programmes.

There are inevitably different opinions within the field on the value of quality assurance, on the most appropriate framework and on the wording of particular standards and criteria. The framework, standards and criteria presented here were developed through extensive consultation with practitioners in the field (see Appendix B). Although we believe practitioners will find them useful, they are presented as guidelines rather than as definitive models. Our hope is that practitioners will critically use these materials as a basis for developing their own quality assurance frameworks and standards.

The materials may be used in any of a number of ways including:

- as a team resource to assist a health promotion unit to develop an explicit quality assurance programme

- as a source of ideas for appropriate standards and criteria for health promotion specialists

- as a resource for reviewing the effectiveness of an existing quality assurance programme

- as a basis of negotiation between health promotion providers and purchasers in agreeing quality standards in contracts

- as a training resource to stimulate thinking and discussion about appropriate approaches to quality assurance in health promotion.

And remember you don't have to do it all at once! Easy guidance on getting started is given in Chapter 4.

Figure 1.1 illustrates one of the possible ways a health promotion manager might use this pack.

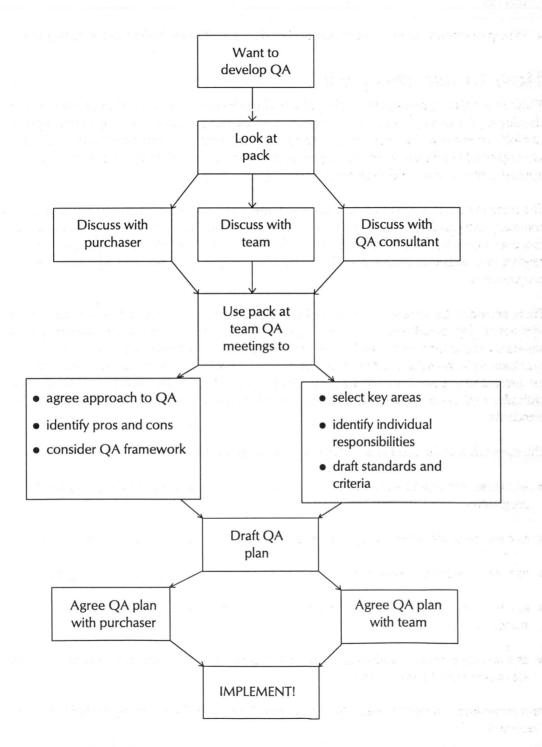

Fig. 1.1. How to use this pack

Quality assurance and health promotion

Attention has been paid to the issue of the quality of health services for a number of years. Since the publication of the White Paper *Working for Patients* (Department of Health, 1989), and the reforms to the NHS which followed it, the issue of quality has been at the top of managerial and professional agendas in the UK. The introduction of purchasing health authorities has given this process further impetus as purchasers seek to establish quality standards in contracting arrangements with service providers. The Patient's Charter initiative has also stimulated action in identifying standards that service users may expect as part of a quality health service. As with any part of the NHS, health promotion providers need to be accountable for the funding they receive, and purchasers need to demonstrate value for money. Figure 1.2 illustrates the many influences contributing to the development of quality assurance in health promotion.

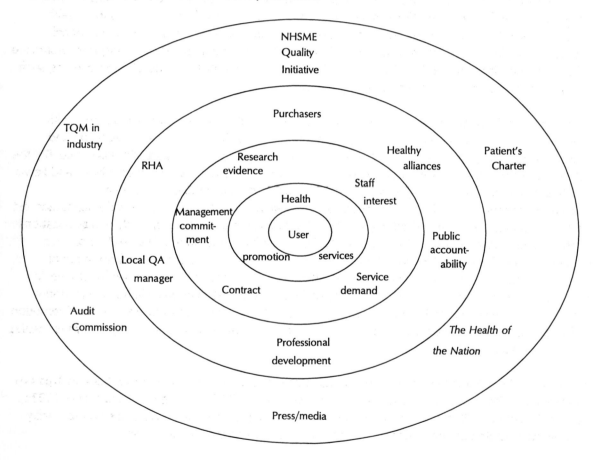

Fig. 1.2. Influences on quality assurance in health promotion

The drive for quality has, however, been bedevilled by a lack of consensus on models, philosophy and terminology. Since 1990 the NHS Executive has advocated an approach to quality called 'Total Quality Management' (TQM) borrowed from industry and which is familiar to many quality assurance specialists (NHS Management Executive, 1992). But despite the appointment of quality assurance managers in many purchasing authorities and provider units, the TQM approach has not always been the basis of health professionals' practice.

There is not even consensus on the use of such common and important terms as 'standard', 'indicator', 'audit' and 'criteria'. 'Audit' is sometimes used to describe the overall process of ensuring quality (as in medical audit), or as one stage in a quality assurance process (as in nursing and other paramedical professions). Within the health promotion field there is not yet an agreed framework or terminology for quality assurance, and there is often uncertainty about the appropriate use of, and the relationship between, outcome indicators and quality indicators.

However, it is also important to recognise the complexity of health promotion work and the limitations of seeking to assess health promotion in purely quantified or cost-benefit terms. There is much of value in health promotion practice which is difficult to quantify and to measure. Health promotion is a dynamic process which may make contributions to user confidence, theoretical understanding, interpersonal skills and strategic vision. It is important, therefore, that quality assurance in health promotion is not reduced to the simplistic counting of only those more visible aspects, such as resource provision, which are more easily measured.

There has been interest for some time in performance and outcome indicators within the health promotion field, and more recently many practitioners and the Society of Health Education and Health Promotion Specialists (SHEPS) have been developing approaches to quality assurance. But the published health promotion literature on quality assurance and audit is very limited. Green and Lewis (1986) summarised the evolving work towards standard setting and the development of measurement tools in the USA. A recent editorial in *Health Promotion International* demonstrated the continued paucity of material (Catford, 1993). In the British literature there are only two publications of note: SHEPS have published *Developing Quality in Health Education and Health Promotion*, a manual with useful material but which does not offer an overall quality assurance framework or provide a practical guide for implementing one (SHEPS, 1992). The report of the Welsh Quality in Health Promotion conference considers many of the issues underlying quality in health promotion, but does not provide a practical manual (MacDonald, 1992). The Dutch Centre for Health Promotion and Health Education has developed and is in the process of implementing a quality system for health promotion (Saan, 1993).

Recently, the NHS Executive has issued national guidance requiring all NHS Authorities and Trusts to provide quality improvement strategies for 1994/95 onwards (NHS Management Executive, 1993a). At a local level this will lead to increased demands for health promotion services to develop quality improvement strategies and to demonstrate progress towards implementing them.

Exercise 1.1

Potential of quality assurance in health promotion

Tick all those items that you think will be of benefit to your practice in health promotion and put a cross against any that you think could be a disadvantage or bring problems.

Clear objectives set ☑

Technical problems ☑

Ability to identify staff development needs ☑

Accountability to the public ☑

Lack of ownership ☑

Provides benchmarks for service development ☑

Basis for negotiation with purchaser ☑

Time-out to reflect on practice ☑

Increases bureaucracy ☑

Measurable indicators used ☑

Value for money ☑

Scope of health promotion practice recognised ☑

Agreed service specification ☑

Time-consuming procedures ☑

Achievement of higher service standards ☑

Consistency of service provision ☑

Better evaluation ☑

Limits scope of activity ☒

Staff satisfaction ☑

Can you think of any other benefits or disadvantages?

Who is this pack designed for?

This pack is primarily designed to be used by health promotion practitioners and their managers in developing and implementing a quality assurance programme within NHS provider health promotion units. It will also be useful for purchasers who wish to contract for quality standards with health promotion providers in an informed and constructive manner.

There is strong evidence from the experience of other professions that for quality assurance in health promotion to be effective, it must be 'owned' by practitioners. Practitioners must feel that quality assurance has some value, and that they are involved in developing appropriate approaches, if it is to have any real impact on improving the quality of their practice. If purchasers or senior managers are too prescriptive in imposing quality assurance frameworks, then practitioners will inevitably adopt a 'tick box' mentality which ensures that they achieve what is required in monitoring terms but does not necessarily lead to any real improvement in quality.

Whilst the standards and criteria apply to the provision of health promotion services, the quality assurance process advocated is one of negotiation and agreement between purchasers and providers, and will require commitment from both parties.

Educationists and students of health promotion should also find the pack of value. Other health promoters including NHS managers, doctors, nurses, environmental health officers and community workers who have health promotion responsibilities as part of their wider role may also find the quality assurance framework and the examples of quality standards useful.

Who has produced this pack?

This pack was produced in the Wessex Regional Health Authority on behalf of the Health Education Authority by a working group led by the Wessex Institute of Public Health Medicine. The working group includes health promotion specialists from both purchasing and providing agencies as well as specialists in public health and quality assurance. The full list of members is given in Appendix B.

Key points

1. Health promotion specialists need to develop quality assurance programmes.
2. There is no one accepted model or framework for quality assurance in health promotion.
3. Quality assurance in health promotion must recognise the different philosophies in the field.
4. Quality assurance programmes need to recognise the value of those aspects of health promotion which are difficult to quantify.
5. Quality assurance must be 'owned' by those who are engaged in health promotion.
6. Health promoters should use this pack as a guide to develop their own quality assurance framework and standards.
7. There needs to be commitment to quality assurance from both the purchasers and providers of health promotion services.

---

2 GOOD PRACTICE IN HEALTH PROMOTION

'Health promotion offers great scope for enhancing the quality of life of populations and individuals alike.'

Summary

This chapter considers the scope of health promotion, examines characteristics of good practice and identifies key functions of health promotion in order to provide a framework for the development of quality standards. After reading this chapter you should be aware of:

1. The scope of health promotion for improving health.

2. Characteristics that reflect good practice in health promotion.

3. The rationale for selecting the six key functions upon which the model quality standards have been developed.

With the greater emphasis on preventing illness and promoting health in recent years, an increasing number of organisations and practitioners have been drawn into the field of health promotion. Whilst this has contributed to the introduction of new ideas and innovation, it has also directed attention to fundamental questions of purpose, objectives, methodology, ethics and outcomes. The issue of quality in health promotion practice is part of such debate since it underpins the action of every practitioner whatever approach is taken in promoting health.

The scope of health promotion

The use of the term 'health promotion' arose in the 1980s from a growing recognition that the determinants of ill health were often to be found in social, economic and environmental conditions such as poverty, unemployment, poor housing and disadvantage in general. The term 'health education' reflected the role of those involved at the time in promoting healthy lifestyles predominantly through strategies aimed at influencing personal behaviour. Whilst health education is an integral part of health promotion, educational approaches alone were seen to be largely ineffective, and so health promotion practice developed to attempt to address the wider determinants of health. Consideration in depth of the definition of health promotion is beyond the scope of this chapter. The World Health Organization (1984) defines health promotion as:

'... the process of enabling people to increase control over, and to improve, their health'.

The approach to developing health promotion policy described in the Ottawa Charter (WHO 1986), identifies the need to:

- build healthy public policy

- create supportive environments

- strengthen community action

- develop personal skills

- reorient health services.

Viewed from a practical perspective, Ewles and Simnett (1992) see health promotion as an umbrella term for a range of activities, including health education, which seek to address the determinants of ill health by operating in various settings. A framework for health promotion is suggested in Figure 2.3.

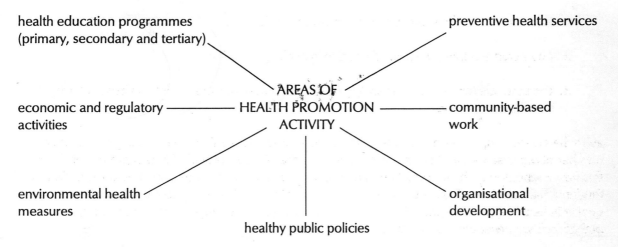

health education programmes
(primary, secondary and tertiary)

preventive health services

AREAS OF
HEALTH PROMOTION
ACTIVITY

economic and regulatory
activities

community-based
work

environmental health
measures

organisational
development

healthy public policies

Fig. 2.3. A framework for health promotion
SOURCE: Ewles and Simnett (1992)

Health promotion is a process in which many people are often involved without necessarily defining their activities as 'health promotion'. This is particularly the case where the focus of attention is upon dimensions of health relating to personal development, emotional issues or interpersonal relationships. Health promotion operates at many levels empowering individuals and communities to resolve difficulties or reach goals deemed to be important to them. Clearly the increasing attention which has been given to the achievement of health gain outcomes will, in no small measure, be dependent upon the effectiveness of these processes.

Health promotion offers great scope for enhancing the quality of life of populations and individuals alike. Its practitioners may be members of the general public, health workers or health promotion specialists, all of whom have a significant contribution to make. The following sections, however, refer particularly to the latter two groups in identifying good practice and the development of quality standards.

Characteristics of good practice

In any discipline there will always be debate and difference of opinion about what constitutes good practice. Nonetheless, we believe that there are specific characteristics of good practice in health promotion, among which are the following:

An agreed philosophy

Those responsible for health promotion should be able to describe the philosophical aspects of what they believe in, what they are trying to do, and some of the guiding principles, as well as the values and ethics, that are involved. Equally they should have shared these thoughts with colleagues and clients in order to arrive at a common understanding of the ideals upon which their activities are based.

A clear vision of health

Models of health have been shown to range from the absence of disease to the concept of self-actualisation or fulfilment. Though an increasing body of opinion now accepts the mental and social dimensions of health, there remains in much of the literature a considerable emphasis upon disease prevention, rather than the promotion of positive health for its own intrinsic value. Health promoters need to share the vision of health in the wider (holistic) sense, with its emphasis upon the positive dimension.

Decisions based on needs assessment

Priority-setting and its subsequent programme development should be based upon the findings of a needs assessment process. Priority-setting in health promotion should rest upon the same criteria as those used for identifying key areas in *The Health of the Nation* (Department of Health, 1992):

1. The area should be a major cause of premature death or avoidable ill health either in the population as a whole or amongst specific groups of people;

2. The area should be one where effective interventions are possible, offering significant scope for improvement in health; and

3. It should be possible to set objectives and targets in the chosen area and monitor progress towards achievement through indicators.

A planned approach

The days of making decisions based upon 'that's a good idea' should be long gone. A planned approach to health promotion activity is essential. This may include an overall health promotion strategy incorporating the philosophical and visionary elements mentioned earlier, or health promotion components of other health strategies. These will identify priorities, objectives, arrangements for monitoring, evaluation and review, allocation of roles, quality assurance and other major aspects of the service to be delivered.

Working in partnerships

No one organisation or sector has the exclusive responsibility for promoting health. In recognising that health itself is a holistic concept and that the determinants of ill health are multi-factorial, it would appear to be both logical and efficient to develop partnerships with those other organisations having both a concern and responsibility for the health of their clients. The joint effort so developed will contribute to a greater output in health terms, provided that partners enter the arena in a positive manner of mutual respect and recognition. The healthy alliances stimulated as a result of *The Health of the Nation* have built upon the WHO Healthy Cities approach and will contribute to the development of detailed action programmes for health promotion based on the participation of all partners.

Strategic leadership

Most successful programmes are able to attribute their success to the existence of strategic leadership in implementing the original concept. Such leadership is essential in convincing key people to become committed to the programme as well as leading the initiative through its various developmental phases towards full implementation.

Realistic aims and claims

Negotiating and stating what health promotion services are able to achieve should be framed realistically, otherwise there is a danger of loss of credibility. This is not to advocate any diminution of ambition or idealism, only to relate our goals to available resources and reasonable outcomes. In an era when services are being judged by 'ability to deliver' it does the profession no service to be perceived or judged by purchasers as failing to achieve. The contractual agreement, therefore, is one requiring considerable thought and negotiation skills if specifications are to be set which will enable completion to the satisfaction of both the purchasing agency and the provider.

Use of effective methods

It is important that health promotion specialists select interventions that are based on research evidence where this is available. Where research evidence is lacking, justifications need to be based on current knowledge of good practice in health promotion, and from the other disciplines from which it is drawn (Bunton and Macdonald, 1992). Explanations may, for instance, refer to group dynamics from the social sciences; to learning theory from educational psychology; or to diffusion theory from communication studies.

Consumer involvement

The contract process has facilitated debate between purchasers and providers on a wide range of issues, as has the development of healthy alliances. Scope still remains, however, for better involvement of users of services, whether the clients are health promoters being helped to promote health more effectively in their occupational role, or members of the general public. Such involvement can be at many levels, ranging from the identification of priorities to the provision of information. The consumer will bring an added dimension to the debate and make it more likely that services will be meeting expressed rather than assumed needs.

Disseminating results

The planning process should give clear indications of the reporting arrangements required of those responsible for major programmes of work. Meticulous record keeping is a good practice in itself but is clearly enhanced if it includes a structured evaluation component. Deadlines enable markers of progress to be established as well as assisting priority setting in the constant resolution of competing demands. Reports are also necessary to inform key personnel of participating organisations and commissioning bodies of the results of their investment in programmes, since accountability is required at every level of practice. Reports should be regarded as a vital aspect of planning, rather than an afterthought or unwelcome chore.

Reflection

Reflection is not just important to practice but also to theory. Health promotion specialists should be able to demonstrate how their services have evolved through experiential learning or the dissemination of good practice by others working in the field. Rather than close our eyes to perceived failure, we should embrace experience as an effective form of learning and be willing to adapt future practice accordingly. Equally we should reflect upon our successes in order to transfer the lessons to other situations which arise in the continuing development of health promotion services.

Motivated and skilled staff

Probably of greatest importance in terms of service provision is the need to employ staff who believe in what they are doing, have a genuine desire to help others, and who possess the necessary personal and professional skills and attributes to do their job well. However good our staff are, if we do not equip or support them properly to deliver quality work, they will not be able to do so. The first point of contact with a department creates a lasting impression with visitors which may not be easily altered if unfavourable. With new demands being made upon services, staff development must be a continuing process if we are to retain the ability to provide high quality services for our clients in future.

From good practice to quality practice

Those examples of good practice to which reference was made earlier are by no means exhaustive but merely indicate some of the ways in which it is possible to demonstrate good standards of work upon which health promotion is based. Where such practices exist then it could be justifiably claimed that a good quality service is being delivered.

Quality has been defined by the British Standards Institution (1978) as:

> '... the totality of the features and characteristics of a product or service that bear on its ability to satisfy stated or implied needs.'

This suggests that quality should be an integral component of the health promotion 'delivered' by practitioners. Quality is not a separate part of the job, it *is* the job.

Exercise 2.1

Characteristics of good practice in health promotion

Decide for yourself or agree as a team which are the three most important characteristics of health promotion, and which three are least important?

	Most important	**Least important**
An agreed philosophy	☐	☐
A clear vision of health	☐	☐
Decisions based on needs assessment	☐	☐
A planned approach	☐	☐
Working in partnership	☐	☐
Strategic leadership	☐	☐
Realistic aims and claims	☐	☐
Use of effective methods	☐	☐
Consumer involvement	☐	☐
Disseminating results	☐	☐
Reflection	☐	☐
Motivated and skilled staff	☐	☐

Are there others that have not been mentioned?

....

....

....

....

....

Exercise 2.2

Characteristics of good practice in health promotion

To what extent does your health promotion practice (either your own or your department's) operate according to these characteristics of good practice?

	Usually	Sometimes	Never
An agreed philosophy	☑	☐	☐
A clear vision of health	☑	☐	☐
Decisions based on needs assessment	☑	☐	☐
A planned approach	☑	☐	☐
Working in partnership	☑	☐	☐
Strategic leadership	☑	☐	☐
Realistic aims and claims	☐	☐	☐
Use of effective methods	☐	☐	☐
Consumer involvement	☑	☐	☐
Disseminating results	☑	☐	☐
Reflection	☑	☐	☐
Motivated and skilled staff	☐	☐	☐

How do your responses compare with the rankings you gave in Exercise 2.1?

....

....

....

....

....

What we are suggesting is that a considerable amount of quality health promotion is already being practised, but that it is not always easy to identify it quickly or demonstrate its existence as part of a structured programme. We are seeking to help you to develop such a programme in order to be able to demonstrate to stakeholders and others the quality of the work performed. Our programme is made up of a quality assurance cycle (described in Chapter 3) and standards based upon important aspects of health promotion (which we call key functions).

Selecting key functions of health promotion for developing quality standards

If quality is to be accepted as an essential component of all health promotion activities, then it is necessary to develop standards that reach the heart of a service or department, rather than be seen as something grafted on at the periphery.

The project team consulted colleagues in order to identify a number of core functions of health promotion for the development of quality standards that could be applied comprehensively by those responsible for providing health promotion. Whilst these may apply to health promotion services in the NHS, local authority or voluntary sector, they primarily reflect important functions of a typical NHS health promotion specialist service. As a result of the consultation exercise, the following six *key functions* were identified as sufficiently broad-based to reflect much health promotion activity, as well as embracing the types of actions taken by health promotion specialists to achieve objectives in various settings and using different methods. So, for example, running a community health fair will involve planning, management, training of staff or volunteers, provision of resources, information and advice, and evaluation of impact.

1. Strategic planning

In recent years there has been a greater acceptance of the need for a more structured approach in planning health promotion, involving the clarification of objectives and pursuit of their achievement through progressive stages of planned activity. Strategic planning is an essential prerequisite of health promotion at all levels of operation, giving direction and shape to every programme or project. Health promotion specialists should also contribute to strategic planning in the context of purchasers' and providers' overall health plans.

2. Programme management

Whether health promotion programmes are organised in terms of issues, settings, client groups or in any other way, it is necessary to ensure that the programme of work is managed efficiently. A planning mechanism should be established with clearly defined and realistic objectives, adequate levels of resources, a timetable of events with deadlines, agreed delegation of tasks and arrangements for review and reporting.

3. Monitoring and evaluation

It is not only important that monitoring and evaluation are undertaken as integral components of all major activities but also that the arrangements for performing them are agreed at the strategic planning stage. Whereas monitoring refers to the assessment of progress in the process of implementing an activity, programme or policy, evaluation is more concerned with the extent to which stated objectives are achieved in terms of impact or outcome measures. Compiling and disseminating reports based upon the findings are also important aspects of these functions. Finally, it is essential that the results of monitoring and evaluation inform future strategic planning.

4. Education and training

With the relative scarcity of resources allocated to health promotion, it is extremely important that impact is maximised by improving the effectiveness of those people in an occupational or social position to promote good health. Planned education and training programmes will contribute to this by providing the necessary information, skills, experience and support for them to be more successful in their role as health promoters.

5. Resources and information

Resources and information are a fundamental aspect of the supportive health promotion services provided, and are an important tool for health promoters. Information may be presented as educational literature, videos or computer programs, or relate to the knowledge of staff as it affects their particular occupational role. All such information must be valid and based upon the principles discussed in Chapter 3.

6. Advice and consultancy

As almost everyone involved in health promotion is called upon to give advice in their area of work, it is important to develop standards for such a function. Since giving advice is closely associated with the broader role of communication it may often be wrongly perceived as something which comes naturally. Advice must be well informed and given in such a way as to be acceptable to the recipient.

Exercise 2.3

Health promotion key functions

Considering your current role, or that of your department or service, could you assign your workload to these key functions? Is there anything that does not seem to fit? Jot down some of your activities under each heading.

(Remember the categories are very broad. For example 'Advice' could be given to a chief executive, health visitor, school child or reporter. 'Resources and information' could be made available to teachers, community groups, or local councillors. 'Education and training' can encompass educational activities undertaken directly with the public and community groups, with field workers and with trainers.)

Strategic planning

Programme management

Monitoring and evaluation

Education and training

Resources and information

Advice and consultancy

Would you add any other functions or change these at all?

....

....

....

....

....

We hope that you agree with our selection of key functions upon which to base quality standards. If however you prefer to identify other functions or activities that you consider to be more relevant to your service then that is fine. The remaining chapters offer a framework and process which is sufficiently flexible to be applied to a wide range of situations and requirements.

Key points

1. Health promotion embraces a wide range of activities in many settings.

2. It is possible and desirable to identify good practice in health promotion.

3. Health promotion practice can be defined in broad functional terms. The six functions used here are: Strategic planning; Programme management; Monitoring and evaluation; Education and training; Resources and information; Advice and consultancy.

4. Quality standards should relate to significant aspects of the role of departments and individuals.

Case study

Health promotion specialist competencies

Maggie Wark of First Community Health has developed a competencies audit involving the following broad areas of activity:

Training and education

Advice and consultancy

Policy development and planning

Raising public awareness

Resources and information

Research.

Participants identify which competencies they are able to provide by completing a grid which requires self-judgement to be made about evidence of competency set against various aspects of the six areas of activity listed above. Subsequent analysis of the audit by the participant and supervisor enables a learning programme to be formulated.

For further details of the scheme contact: Maggie Wark, Director of Health Promotion, First Community Health, Mellow House, Corporation Street, Stafford ST16 3SR.

Case study

Competencies for professional development in health education

The Health Education Authority is currently funding a project at the Cheltenham and Gloucester College of Higher Education to develop competencies in health education and health promotion. The objectives of the project are to:

- identify competencies for different professional groups and levels of responsibility in health education and health promotion

- develop methods of competency measurement and assessment

- identify education and training opportunities which will develop competencies in health education and health promotion

- develop national management strategies for quality assurance in health education, health promotion, education and training.

Contact: Elizabeth Rolls, Competencies for Professional Development in Health Education, Department of Social and Community Studies, Cheltenham and Gloucester College of Higher Education, The Park Campus, The Park, Cheltenham GL50 2QF. Tel: 0242 532874.

3 QUALITY ASSURANCE IN HEALTH PROMOTION

'The development of a quality assurance programme will contribute to the development of a quality health promotion service.'

Summary

This chapter offers a definition of quality assurance in health promotion and suggests a rationale for developing a quality assurance programme. After reading this chapter you should be able to:

1. Describe quality assurance in health promotion.

2. Identify appropriate methods for ensuring quality in health promotion.

3. Identify the resources and support you will need to develop quality assurance.

4. Begin to plan your own quality assurance programme.

What is quality assurance in health promotion?

Chapter 2 sought to define quality in terms of good practice in health promotion. Turning from more general principles of health promotion to practical programmes for assessing and improving quality, there is a need to define not only quality, but also what is meant by 'quality assurance'.

There is no single agreed definition of quality assurance. We have chosen to work with the following definition of quality assurance in health promotion:

Quality assurance is a systematic process through which achievable and desirable levels of quality are described, the extent to which these levels are achieved is assessed, and action is taken following assessment to enable them to be reached. (Adapted from Wright and Whittington, 1992)

Quality assurance therefore describes an integrated series of activities including:

- deciding to develop a quality assurance programme

- identifying the key areas for a quality assurance programme

- setting standards

- agreeing criteria to measure standards

- measuring performance

- taking action to improve quality

- regular review.

The key is that these activities are part of a planned and systematic attempt to improve the quality of a service. It should be noted that quality and quality assurance do not necessarily go together. One may have a quality health promotion service without a quality assurance programme. One may even have a quality assurance programme and not have a quality health promotion service. However, our argument is that the development of a quality assurance programme will contribute to the development of a quality health promotion service.

The distinctions between quality assurance and other forms of systematic investigation in health promotion such as research, needs assessment and outcome evaluation are not always clear. There are often no easy dividing lines between these related approaches, but in practice it is possible to make some useful distinctions. For example, quality assurance should be an integral and continuing part of health promotion practice while research activity is usually a more discrete and time-limited project. Needs assessment is a stage in the planning process while quality assurance should be applied to the whole process. Quality assurance is ultimately concerned with outcomes but in the first instance is concerned with structures and processes. We offer definitions of these terms in the glossary (Appendix D), but suggest you think through their similarities and differences in Exercise 3.1.

Case study

Bath Health Promotion Unit system for monitoring projects and improving evaluation

Bath Health Promotion Unit was interested in designing a system to monitor its major projects and improve the quality and extent of their evaluation. It was thought that the information gained from the system would be useful to both the purchasers and to the unit. The purchasers would be interested in the cost and efficacy of the projects and the unit could use the evaluation findings to improve its methods and efficiency. In particular it was thought useful to be able to comment on the costings of the project in terms of staff time and use of resources.

The system has been developed over the last two years and is now in use for all major projects within the unit.

The system has three components which can be represented as shown in Figure 3.1.

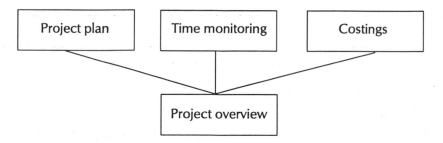

Fig. 3.1. System devised by Bath Health Promotion Unit

The project plan is compiled at the outset and describes the nature of the project. Its main features are:

- a short overview of the project

- defined aims and objectives

- detailed timescales using commercially available software

- specification of how the project will be evaluated in terms of input, process, output and outcome

- to provide details of relevant computer files and documents

- to refer to the unit's contract with the purchaser

- to anchor the project to Health of the Nation targets.

The time monitoring component records the time spent on projects across the whole unit and relies upon the use of commercially available software.

Each member of staff completes a weekly time sheet recording the time spent on different projects and the activities within those projects by key area, topic area and target group.

Figure 3.2 displays this structure and gives an example.

Costings

The software allows summations to be readily made across these categories, not just on projects or individuals; the time spent working in particular key areas, topic areas or target groups is therefore accessible. As the hourly rate of individuals is known, the overall staff cost for each project may be obtained using the software; similarly costings by any category are possible. Non-staff costs are also recorded.

Structure	Example
Individual __ __ __ __ __ __ __ __	Individual A
Key area __ __ __ __ __ __ __ __ __	CHD
Topic area __ __ __ __ __ __ __ __ __	Smoking
Project __ __ __ __ __ __ __ __ __ __	Smoking in pregnancy
Target group __ __ __ __ __ __ __ __ __	NHS
Activity __ __ __ __ __ __ __ __ __ __	Planning

Category	Examples
Key areas	HIV/AIDS, CHD, accident prevention
Topic areas	sexual health, drug prevention, smoking, alcohol, physical activity
Target groups	education, social services, NHS, voluntary organisations, industry and commerce
Activities	administration, planning, meetings, travelling, report writing and training

Fig. 3.2. What is recorded

Summary

Whilst the system requires commitment and effort from staff the benefits are many:

- it helps to clarify the nature of the project

- it identifies milestones and timescales

- the evaluation process is clarified and in place before the project commences

- the project plan aids the report writing process

- accurate costings are produced

- the project plan is a good tool in negotiations and creates a good image

- recording identifiable elements and stages within the project will aid future audit.

For more information contact: Mike Brewin, Bath Health Promotion Unit, District Headquarters, Newbridge Hill, Bath BA1 3QE. Tel: 0225 313640.

Exercise 3.1

Characteristics of quality assurance, needs assessment, outcome evaluation and research

Place 'Y' or 'N' in each column to indicate whether you agree or disagree that the term has the characteristic indicated.

Characteristic	Quality assurance	Needs assessment	Output evaluation	Research
Systematic				
Concerned with ultimate effectiveness				
Continuous				
Everyone's responsibility				
One stage in the planning process				
Integral to every aspect of HP				
Needs to involve service users				
May use a variety of methods				
May be a time-limited one-off project				

Compare your four columns. Are there significant difference between them? What does this tell you about QA?

Quality assurance and audit

Currently there are a number of different approaches, frameworks and models that could be applied to quality assurance in health promotion. Some practitioners choose to define their approach to quality using the term 'audit' while others prefer quality assurance. 'Audit' has been defined by SHEPS as the 'systematic, critical analysis of the quality of health promotion programmes and services' (1992). Used in this way we believe that audit is synonymous with quality assurance. We prefer to use the term quality assurance as audit is sometimes also used in the more narrow sense of the review and assessment stage in a quality assurance process.

We have provided a glossary of terms used (see Appendix D) in order to move towards a consistent and clear usage of terms. It is recommended that you also provide a glossary of terms used in your quality assurance programme, and use them consistently in any planning documents and reports.

Case study

The Society of Health Education and Promotion Specialists audit scheme

- One of the society's key functions is to help develop and promote standards of good practice in health promotion. Towards this end, the society has produced a Code of Conduct for all members and registered specialists. Also, the society has produced its own 'Developing quality in health education and health promotion' which includes a classification of indicators for evaluating practice. It is appropriate for the profession to promote an egalitarian approach to quality assurance, to make it easier for all practitioners to understand how to assess their work. However, self-assessment is only one element of a process which should include peer audit, organisational development and change.

- In 1991 a group of health promotion specialists who volunteered an interest, met together to explore how they could offer to help other specialist teams to audit their practice. The group agreed that their role would not be to assess how well or how poorly services were performing, and could not offer sustained help to develop services, or act as an arbitrator to resolve differences. What they focused upon was a clear framework to help classify the mechanisms which departments/teams had established and could establish to audit their performance.

- This framework was developed into a set of guidelines for use by an experienced health promotion specialist who had received additional training on the guidelines. The guidelines were designed to reflect good practice back to the informant and to expose any weaknesses, deficiencies, or inconsistencies in the systems available to set and monitor standards.

- Following the publication of the guidelines and initial training, the scheme has been running informally, with requests for audit visits being referred to one of a list of trained auditors. The focus of each audit is agreed between participants, along with practical arrangements and any costs to be levied. The auditor and auditee are asked to provide a brief report for quality monitoring and training purposes.

- In 1993 the society decided to review the operation of the scheme and decide whether it could be improved upon, and how it could operate. A small working group, covered by the society's deputy chair, has begun work on this task and is expected to report to the executive in 1994. It is likely that the society will want to continue to offer professional guidance on audit in some form.

- A selection of questions from the society's audit guidelines follows:

Issues for audit

Structural issues:	Resources
	Organisational framework
	Policy and planning framework
	Information and communication
Programme issues:	Planning process
	Aims and objectives
	Input, process and outcomes
	Evaluation, monitoring and follow-up.

For any or all of these issues, the auditor could consider relevant quality aspects, namely:

effectiveness	service standards
efficiency	acceptability
appropriateness	equity
range	adherence to code of practice.

For more information on the scheme, please contact: Brian Neeson, Deputy Chair, Society of Health Education and Promotion Specialists. Tel: 0256 312252.

Ensuring quality in health promotion

The stages in the model of a quality assurance cycle for health promotion are described below. But first we want to ask several important questions that you need to consider before initiating a quality assurance programme. What methods do you already have for ensuring a quality service in health promotion? What are the aims of your quality assurance programme? Who should be involved? And what principles should you base your programme on?

In developing a quality assurance programme you will almost certainly want to begin by considering what methods you already have for ensuring quality. In most cases quality assurance systems should pull together and build upon rather than replace existing processes for ensuring quality. If you are just beginning to develop a quality assurance programme, you probably have more methods and resources for ensuring quality than you realise.

When asked about their methods for ensuring quality, health promotion practitioners gave a wide range of answers, some of which we list here:

- practice based on research

- employment of staff with professional qualifications

- user satisfaction surveys

- professional code of conduct

- good staff morale

- health promotion charters

- adoption of British Standard 5750

- peer audit

- management techniques (individual performance review, etc.)

- programme evaluation

- contract monitoring reports.

Note that not all of these aspects can or should feature in a quality assurance programme. Some factors are important but not easily measurable. Quality assurance is concerned with the development of a system which relates to that which is both desirable and measurable.

Exercise 3.2

Methods for ensuring quality

Considering your own practice, do you use any of the methods for ensuring quality listed below? Tick those that apply.

	Sometimes	Usually
Practice based on research	☐	☐
Employment of staff with professional qualifications	☐	☐
User satisfaction surveys	☐	☐
Professional code of conduct	☐	☐
Maintaining good staff morale	☐	☐
Health promotion charters	☐	☐
Adoption of British Standard 5750	☐	☐
Peer audit	☐	☐
Management techniques (individual performance review , etc.)	☐	☐
Programme evaluation	☐	☐
Contract monitoring reports	☐	☐

Case study

Positive Action

Positive Action is the HIV prevention section of Somerset Health Authority. After researching various quality initiatives, mainly in industry, the importance of involving all staff in developing standards was identified as essential to the success of any scheme.

The process started by borrowing a number of short videos on quality from the Department of Trade and Industry (DTI) and generating discussion about the issues. A day was then designated for developing quality standards and the office was closed to enable all staff to attend. The venue was the home of one staff member to create an informal atmosphere. Staff were asked to explore their perceptions of the strengths and weaknesses in the system, and what improvements and monitoring might be done effectively without greatly increasing the administrative workload.

The first step was to define what was meant by quality standards, and some time was spent discussing the various standards defined by the DTI, British Standards Institution and the International Standards Organisation. The meaning of 'quality' as opposed to 'quality assurance' was also clarified.

A 'mission statement' was developed, to which all staff contributed. Having agreed a direction, then each aspect of work was examined. It was agreed that many of the current weaknesses stemmed from a lack of good office practice and misunderstandings of the role of other members of staff. The discussion naturally evolved into how these could best be eliminated. Out of the discussion arose a number of 'rules' which if adhered to would ensure the smooth running of the various systems.

The new system was introduced on an agreed day, with the weeks before that used to pilot monitoring arrangements, and an agreement reached to have 'quality weeks' when the monitoring systems would be reviewed. Three months later the first such week took place. All office, telephone and letter contacts were summarised, with 5 per cent sent a questionnaire. From responses, further areas of concern were identified. This response was then used to obtain additional staffing, which aims to reduce the difficulties identified.

Although most of the first set of standards revolved around administration, quality principles are now being extended outward into staff development and training. At the outset there was some staff resistance to the idea of anything regarding quality, with staff concerned about possible job losses. The reality has proved quite different. Those members of staff particularly resistant mentioned that the quality day had completely altered their perception regarding this work, and felt much more positive and committed.

For more information contact: Diane Scorer, District HIV Prevention Co-ordinator, Somerset Health Authority, Wellspring Road, Taunton TA2 7PQ. Tel: 0823 333491.

The rationale for quality assurance

Ultimately the purpose of a quality assurance programme in health promotion will be to contribute to the achievement of positive health outcomes. One possible distinction between quality assurance and outcome evaluation is that quality assurance is directly concerned with health promotion structures and processes, and only indirectly concerned with outcomes. Thus the ultimate goal of quality assurance is to increase health gain for the population served by the health promotion service; but the immediate aim of a quality assurance programme is to facilitate the continual improvement in the quality of health promotion services.

The complex and long-term nature of most health promotion interventions makes it difficult to prove whether achieving this improvement in service quality will lead to the ultimate goal of health gain. Further research certainly needs to be done on this question. In the mean time practitioners need to make judgements as to whether they believe quality assurance programmes are likely to lead to health gain on the basis of the available evidence. Although there is little in the wider health care quality assurance literature to demonstrate the link conclusively, the experience of other industries provides strong evidence that quality assurance is cost effective (Ellis and Whittington, 1993).

Who should be involved in quality assurance?

Quality assurance should be 'owned' by health promotion managers and practitioners rather than by purchasers and senior managers. Unless quality assurance has meaning and value for practitioners it is unlikely that they will have the commitment necessary to make it work. We would further argue that it will be most effective if approached as a team rather than by individual practitioners. This does not mean that everyone need have the same degree of responsibility. It might well be useful to have one manager or practitioner identified as a quality assurance co-ordinator who facilitates a quality assurance programme involving the rest of the team.

Clearly purchasers and senior managers also have a role in requiring some sort of quality framework and specifying monitoring and reporting arrangements. Others may also be usefully involved in the process including quality assurance/audit specialists. User involvement, defined both in terms of those other workers and agencies who often 'use' health promotion services and of individual users in the community, is also important. Figure 3.4 illustrates the range of stakeholders who might be involved.

Who you involve depends of course on availability, and on your personal experience and organisational structure. It is worth thinking early in the process about who might make a contribution to your quality assurance programme.

Exercise 3.3

Contributions from stakeholders to a quality assurance programme

Can you identify individuals from the following list of stakeholders who could be involved in developing your quality assurance programme? Think about which of these should be responsible for leading the programme, and what contributions you might expect the others to make. How enthusiastic are they likely to be?

	Name	Contribution
Quality assurance manager	....	....
Provider contracts manager	....	....
Health promotion manager	....	....
Purchaser health promotion specialist	....	....
Health promotion specialists	....	....
Director of purchasing/contracting	....	....
Public health consultant	....	....
Service user(s)	....	....
Medical audit advisory group	....	....
Society of Health Promotion and Health Education Specialists (SHEPS)	....	....
Others	....	....

Principles of quality assurance in health promotion

Ultimately, any form of quality assurance is based on a set of values, and in health promotion these values may be defined in terms of a set of core principles (adapted from Maxwell, 1984) as follows:

- equity – that users have equal access to and/or equal benefit from services

- effectiveness – that services achieve their intended objectives

- efficiency – that services achieve maximum benefit for minimum cost

- accessibility – that a service is easily available to users in terms of time, distance and ethos

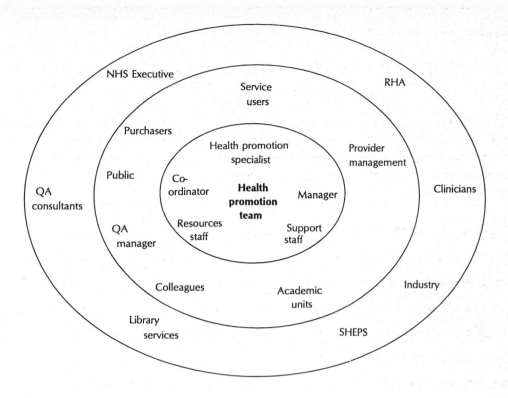

Fig. 3.4. Who should be involved in quality assurance?

- appropriateness – that a service is that which the users require

- acceptability – that services satisfy the reasonable expectations of users

- responsiveness – that services address the expressed needs of users.

The standards and criteria suggested in Appendix A are intended to reflect these fundamental principles; we recommend that any standards and criteria you devise should also be based on and tested against these principles.

Implications of quality assurance

The implications of quality assurance for providers and purchasers will be discussed more fully in Chapters 4 and 5. For the moment we simply wish to note the possible costs as well as benefits of quality assurance. The introduction of quality assurance is intended to improve the quality of health promotion services provided, but it must be recognised that it will almost inevitably have both costs and benefits. Benefits have been considered in Chapter 1, but potential costs may include time-consuming procedures, reallocation of resources away from direct service provision and the creation of a 'tick box' mentality.

However, the existing costs of poor quality also need to be counted. Most health promotion specialists can cite examples of programmes where poor planning or poor management led to the inefficient use of resources. Even in the best run services there will be some scope for improvement. If quality assurance is approached as a process with costs as well as benefits, which is designed to achieve the greatest improvement for the least cost, then it is hard to imagine that the net effect will not be beneficial. Any decision not to introduce quality assurance needs to be justified just as rigorously as a decision to do so. Quality assurance is not a panacea; it is a practical approach to identifying areas for improvement in health promotion practice and working towards that improvement in an explicit and systematic way.

Establishing a quality assurance programme will require time, commitment and resources. But it need not be difficult. You do not have to do everything at once! You can begin with gradual change, phased in over time. The step-by-step guide to this is in Chapter 4.

The quality assurance cycle

Quality assurance by definition requires a process of description and assessment of standards. It is also crucial that the process be explicit and systematic. The whole process of quality assurance is most commonly described as a cycle. It can be described in many different ways, but we have chosen to identify the following six-stage quality assurance cycle (adapted from Ellis and Whittington, 1993):

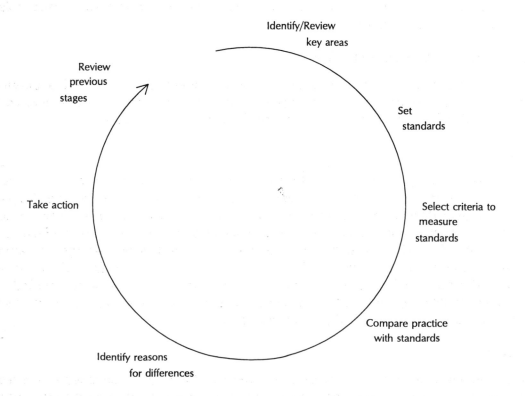

Fig. 3.5 Quality assurance cycle

1. Identify/review key areas for quality assurance

Time and other constraints will necessitate the identification of a limited number of key areas for quality assurance. These may be identified in terms of *programme areas* (HIV and sexual health, coronary heart disease, women's health), *settings* (education, community), *localities* or key health promotion *functions*. Agreement should be sought within the health promotion team as to what key areas will be identified and who should be involved in the quality assurance process (Exercise 3.4). We have chosen to develop our model using the six key *functions* (strategic planning, programme management, monitoring and evaluation, education and training, resources and information, and advice and consultancy) described in Chapter 2, as our key areas.

2. Set standards

A standard defines an agreed level of performance, which might range from 'satisfactory' to 'excellent'. One or more standards should be set for each key area. The standard should be set in a standard statement which is an agreed level of performance and relevant to the key area. A standard statement should be concise, clearly written and acceptable to relevant colleagues and service users. Agreement should also be sought on who is to be involved in the setting of standards and criteria.

3. Select criteria to measure standards

Criteria should specify clearly and precisely the levels of performance which have to be achieved to satisfy the standard, and the method of measurement. Criteria should be achievable, measurable, observable, understandable and reasonable.

4. Compare practice with standards

Consideration needs to be given to when the criteria will be measured: retrospectively at the end of a programme or at predetermined stages in the programme? There will need to be a discussion of who will be involved in the comparison: users, practitioners, managers, colleagues?

5. Take action

The action taken will depend on the results of the preceding stage. If practice does not meet the standards, the reasons for the differences need to be assessed. This is necessarily a subjective process but should be guided by the team. Once the reasons for the differences have been agreed the team should plan for changes to the health promotion programme to ensure that the standard is met in the future. It might of course be realised that the standards were not realistic or meaningful and action may need to be taken to identify more useful standards. If the standards were fully achieved it may be that the standards need to be raised, or that new more rigorous standards should be identified. Alternatively it might be appropriate to consider standards in a wholly new area of practice. In either case the effect is to lead to a continuing improvement in quality.

6. Review

At a predetermined time in the planning cycle, the preceding stages should be reviewed to assess if they have been successfully completed and, if not, whether appropriate planning and action have been taken to address the situation. The review could be undertaken by the team (at an annual planning and review meeting), by the practitioner/programme manager or by an outside peer auditor

(SHEPS, 1992). Whatever the result of stage 5 some action should have been taken and the team will need to review and reflect on the aims, methods and key areas of their quality assurance programme.

Exercise 3.4

Identifying key areas for quality assurance

Discuss with your team which key areas to use for your quality assurance programme.

Consider the pros and cons of using programme areas, settings, localities or functions for the development of quality standards

	Advantages	Disadvantages
Programmes		
Settings		
Localities		
Functions		
Other		

Key points

1. Quality assurance involves a planned and systematic attempt to improve quality.
2. Quality assurance relates to that which is both desirable and measurable.
3. Quality assurance should involve key stakeholders including service users.
4. Quality assurance is based on core principles – equity, effectiveness, efficiency, accessibility, appropriateness, acceptability and responsiveness.
5. Quality assurance is a cycle which includes identifying key areas, setting standards and criteria, comparing practices with standards, identifying reasons for differences, taking action and reviewing previous stages.

4 GETTING STARTED – GUIDELINES FOR PROVIDERS

'Accept that you cannot do everything at once. Begin with a few key areas.'

Summary

This chapter is designed to help you, as a practitioner or manager of a health promotion service, make a start at introducing a structured quality assurance programme to your department. It also describes the assessment protocol designed for use with the standards illustrated. After reading this chapter you should:

1. Be clearer about why you wish to develop a programme.

2. Have decided how you will introduce the proposal for a programme to your team.

3. Have given some thought to key areas for the development of quality standards.

4. Be familiar with the use of an assessment protocol.

5. Be familiar with the examples of standards.

Planning a quality assurance programme

It is important that you are clear in your own mind about why you wish to introduce a quality assurance programme into your department. As was stated in Chapter 3 there are both costs and benefits that need to be given careful consideration. It is also essential that all the members of the team are convinced of the value of giving time and effort to the programme.

In order to help guide you through the various stages of developing a quality assurance programme, a number of checklists for action follow. You may wish to use these to note action points and progress made.

There are three key points to emphasise in order to plan a structured quality assurance programme:

- Allow for a full discussion about the plans for a programme with your team

- Allocate overall responsibility for the programme

- Be selective and realistic in its implementation.

Case study

Dorset quality assurance plan

Dorset Health Promotion Service started by designating a senior member of staff to be responsible for quality assurance. This led to a draft quality assurance plan, based upon district and regional guidelines, being developed and presented for comment at a staff meeting. The plan was later sent to the Health Commission's Quality Manager for further comment before being accepted as the department's formal plan for assuring quality.

The quality assurance specialist then arranged to meet with other members of staff in small groups to discuss the rationale for developing quality standards as part of a departmental quality assurance programme. Such meetings were very important in:

1. Reassuring staff that the programme would help them deliver quality health promotion

2. Focusing attention upon the key aspects of each person's role

3. Preparing the groundwork for agreement on departmental and personal quality standards.

Having raised awareness of the development of a structured quality assurance programme the next phase will be guided by this national project in agreeing standards for all members of staff. At the time of writing the intention is to combine the review of these standards with other forms of assessment (e.g. individual performance review) though there may be certain disadvantages if the quality assurance programme is perceived as being 'owned' and imposed by the management tier. We very much wish to see ownership clearly in the hands of practitioners who accept the contribution of such a programme to the achievement of their own personal goals and aspirations.

For further information contact: Dr Mike Head, Public Health Promotion, Dorset Health Commission, Victoria House, Princes Road, Ferndown, Dorset BH22 9JR. Tel: 0202 893000.

Hold a workshop for your team to explore and agree some of the major issues involved (see 'How to use this pack', Figure 1.1, p. 3). This could cover:

- the perceived benefits and costs

- the purpose of the programme

- the major components

- the procedures to be completed

- an estimate of the workload

- the impact upon health promotion practice

- arrangements for reporting and review.

A workshop should help convince all team members that they will benefit from the introduction of a programme, and will contribute to their feeling of 'ownership' of the programme.

Some may have reservations about what may appear to be another form of inspection of performance. It is important that they are reassured that the quality assurance programme is designed to demonstrate the high quality of aspects of their role as well as to identify the help required to achieve other agreed standards.

Having made a start at introducing your quality assurance programme it is essential that its momentum be maintained. The co-ordinator has a vital role to play in developing standards, reviewing practice and ensuring that the quality assurance cycle (Figure 3.5) continues to revolve as planned. The programme will be developmental, gradually becoming more ambitious in the light of achievement of its initial goals.

Checklist 1

Thinking about quality assurance

You may find it helpful to seek answers to these questions; refer back to Chapter 3.

1. Why do you wish to introduce a planned quality assurance programme?
2. Are you convinced of its benefits?
3. What are the costs (in all senses) of its introduction?
4. How do you feel that your staff will react to it?
5. How will you convince staff that they will benefit from its introduction?
6. Does your organisation have someone with special responsibility for quality assurance?
7. If so, have you discussed the progress of quality assurance recently?
8. Does your employer have a quality assurance policy?
9. Does your organisation have any written statement about standards?
10. How will a quality assurance programme help your department to thrive?

Checklist 2

Planning for quality assurance

1. Decide who is going to co-ordinate your quality assurance programme. This will be a substantial task and should, therefore, be recognised as a major objective for that person.
2. Discuss and negotiate your expectations with the co-ordinator (if it isn't you). Make it quite clear to the co-ordinator what you see to be the benefits of a quality assurance programme.
3. Consider what support and resources you and your team will need to develop your quality assurance programme.
4. Make arrangements to discuss your plans with your staff.
5. Accept that you cannot do everything at once. Begin with a few key areas.
6. Draw up an outline plan of your proposed quality assurance programme showing the main components and future timetable of events.
7. Consider how you might evaluate the impact of your quality assurance programme.
8. Consider how you might involve clients or users in your quality assurance programme.

Checklist 3

Introducing your quality assurance programme

These are some of the steps that people have found useful and which you may wish to consider:

1. Exploring the benefits for the department and the individual of developing such a programme.
2. Discussing the pressures on managers to demonstrate both the quality and effectiveness of services commissioned.
3. Convincing your team that you regard quality assurance as a vital aspect of your department's role.
4. Reassuring staff regarding any perceived threat to them from this initiative.
5. Explaining that it presents an opportunity to convince stakeholders of your department's high standards of performance.
6. Having introduced your ideas, allowing time to reflect upon the opportunities.
7. Giving some thought to differentiating between departmental standards for everyone and personal standards for individuals.

8. Involving staff in identifying and agreeing those important aspects of their role that would benefit from the development of standards.

9. Ensuring that standards for all staff are agreed and written.

10. Producing a quality assurance report which contains your programme and all standards agreed for the department and individuals.

The quality assurance cycle recommended in Chapter 3 for adoption includes the setting of standards and associated criteria. Such standards may relate to a wide range of functions including contact with clients. The following case study illustrates how standards have been developed for GPs and primary healthcare teams.

Case study

Developing standards

Oxfordshire FHSA, in conjunction with Oxfordshire Community Unit, has published a guidance pack on the primary healthcare charter for GP and primary healthcare teams.

The pack includes a sheet on each primary healthcare standard area and details an Oxfordshire example of good practice. Local standards have been recommended in three areas: access to members of the primary healthcare team in an emergency, urgently, routinely, and by telephone; obtaining a repeat prescription; and using a practice-based complaints procedure. The standards are based on existing, unwritten policies and examples of best practice. They represent core standards which the FHSA encourages all practices to meet.

In the coming year, practices are being encouraged to draw up a list of standards which they will publicise to patients via waiting room notices and through their practice leaflets. The FHSA and community unit have held five roadshows around the county publicising the charter to practice and community unit staff. These events will be followed up with seminars for practice managers on practice-based complaints procedures and workshops on other charter initiatives.

The standards are being monitored continuously and an audit report will be produced in two years. The quarterly Patient's Charter monitoring exercise will provide information on the development of local standards and practice charters.

For further details contact: Alison Campbell, Patient Services Officer, Oxfordshire FHSA, Headington OX3 7LG. Tel: 0865 226546.

Checklist 4

Maintaining your quality assurance programme

1. Agree a timetable for putting your quality assurance cycle into practice.
2. Arrange for the co-ordinator to see individuals to 'compare practice with standards' (stage 4 of the cycle).
3. Consider how you might combine (or integrate) your quality assurance cycle with individual performance review or any other formal assessment protocol currently used in your department.
4. Recognise the development and adoption of personal standards as a major objective for all staff involved in a formal assessment system.
5. Raise and review your quality assurance programme at a meeting of all staff twice annually.
6. Review the role of the quality assurance co-ordinator.

Developing your own quality standards

The quality assurance cycle described in Chapter 3 included (stage 2) 'the process of setting standards' and (stage 3) 'the selection of criteria to measure such standards'. We also described in Chapter 2 the rationale for the six key functions upon which our standards are based.

If you wish to develop your own standards then you need to:

- establish a standard setting group

- identify your key area/function for which standards will be developed

- set your standards

- agree the criteria which demonstrate the standards.

Establish a standard setting group

The group should comprise not more than six and, ideally, not less than four people. It could include someone from 'beyond' the health promotion team if the individual has special interests, qualities or experience. The key area(s) identified for standard setting would clearly influence the composition of the group. The length and frequency of meetings will need to be determined whilst bearing in mind continuity, other commitments and the agreed schedule of work.

Identify the key areas (or functions)

These key areas should reflect major dimensions of health promotion practice in order that the ensuing standards are accepted as relevant to major daily activity. Our key areas are generic functions that, in the main, may be related to all staff. You may prefer, however, to use a different classification in identifying key areas such as specific programmes or settings. It is for you (or your group) to determine what you consider to be most appropriate for your department as suggested in Exercise 3.4.

Setting standards

Once a key area has been identified the next stage is to construct appropriate standards. One way to make a start would be to answer the questions:

- What is it about this key area that is important?

- What are the major components of this key area?

Having identified a small number of important aspects of the key area there are two suggested ways forward:

(a) Each person constructs a statement about one aspect to reflect the existence of good quality practice. The group then discuss each person's standard statement and modify it if necessary. If members were briefed beforehand about the group's task, each person could give some prior thought to the construction of personal or departmental standards.

or

(b) The full group work together throughout on a standard for each aspect.

Agreeing criteria

Criteria are the detailed indicators of the standard. They may be phrased as statements of practice which provide evidence that the standard is being addressed. Quality standards in some disciplines phrase their criteria in the form of questions, the answers to which help support or reject the attainment of the standard.

The standard setting group may again choose to work collectively or individually on the construction of criteria as for the standard statements. Both standards and their associated criteria may need several phases of re-wording in the light of further discussion and reflection even in the early formative stages. This is a normal part of the process and will, in fact, enhance the quality of the group's work.

Applying the standards based upon our key functions

Standards such as those developed in this document (see Appendix A) need to be applied to the working practices and procedures established by health promotion practitioners. These practices vary and may be based upon issues (programmes), settings (for example, schools), client groups, functions (for example, training) or other categories. One way of considering the application of these standards would be to decide whether you wish to assess quality across the department (for example, planning) or quality in relation to key programmes of work such as those highlighted in *The Health of the Nation* or local strategy documents. If the focus is primarily upon key functions throughout the department then the appropriate standards (such as monitoring and evaluation) would be addressed 'vertically' across all staff involved in the various programmes within a department.

Exercise 4.1

Organising quality assurance to fit your department

Think about the organisation of your department or service. How would you organise your quality assurance programme – across key functions or programme areas or a combination of both? Can you identify a member of staff who would take the lead for each approach? Note their names in the matrix section.

Key area / Programme	Strategic planning	Programme management	Monitoring and evaluation	Education and training	Resources and information	Advice and consultancy
Cardiovascular						
Mental health						
Sexual health						
Smoking						
LAYH						
Accidents						
Substance misuse						
Other						

On the other hand you may wish to examine the overall quality of a particular programme (for example, Accidents) and proceed by applying the full range of standards 'horizontally' (across all six key functions) to the programme in question.

Various combinations of both approaches are also possible.

The next steps would be to continue by applying stages 5 and 6 of the quality assurance cycle (Chapter 3) following this department-wide assessment.

Although we suggest that you plan your quality assurance in these sorts of achievable 'chunks', and select the standards and criteria that you will use to assess them, this is simply to help you start. The six key functions and the model standards and criteria are intended to encompass the breadth of health promotion activity. The quality of a health promotion service will be measured by this breadth, as well as by excellence in particular aspects. So if you start small, bear in mind that you will need to broaden the scope of your quality assurance programme as it develops.

The assessment protocol

An important aspect of the quality assurance process is the mechanism by which standards will be assessed. The protocol designed for the assessment of standards in this document is shown in Figure 4.1.

[1] Function 1.   Strategic planning

[2] Standard 1.1   There is a group which addresses strategic planning issues in health promotion

[3] Assessor .... Date of assessment............................

[4] Criteria	[5] Assessment method	[6] Level of achievement 1–5	[7] Completion date	[8] Comments/ Action required

Level of achievement code: 1 = Fully achieved 2 = Substantial progress 3 = Partly achieved 4 = Work has commenced 5 = No progress

Fig. 4.1. Form for assessing standards in quality assurance

The steps for completion of the assessment protocol are as follows:

[1.] Function

The appropriate key function is inserted as shown (e.g. Strategic planning). A number has been allocated to functions, standards and criteria for identification purposes.

[2.] Standard

The appropriate standard statement is recorded beneath the function.

[3.] Assessor

Details of the person undertaking the assessment should be inserted, together with the date of the assessment. The assessor may be one of several people depending upon the type of use being made of these materials. The assessment may be undertaken internally, by peer review or in conjunction with an external agent such as a commissioning authority. The details of the assessor will, therefore, need to be completed at the time of the exercise and will clearly vary from one situation to another.

[4.] Criteria

[4]	[5]	[6]	[7]	[8]
Criteria (Example)	Assessment method	Level of achievement 1–5	Completion date	Comments/Action required
The group has agreed terms of reference.				

A set of criteria has been developed for each standard. These criteria provide evidence of actions which indicate that the standard is being addressed.

[5.] Assessment method

[4]	[5]	[6]	[7]	[8]
Criteria (Example)	Assessment method	Level of achievement 1–5	Completion date	Comments/Action required
The group has agreed terms or reference.	Review programme planning documents			

This column requires the provider to identify in advance the method to be used in demonstrating that the criterion has been achieved. By so doing the materials can be used as part of a forward-planning process as well as in departmental review. Among the range of demonstration methods would be:

- observation

- review meetings

- review planning documents

- individual performance review

- review departmental reports

- survey of clients or partners (in alliances)

- records of activities.

An external assessor may then be directed to the appropriate documentation in order to verify the attainment of criteria if required.

[6.] Level of achievement

[4]	[5]	[6]	[7]	[8]
Criteria (Example)	Assessment method	Level of achievement 1–5	Completion date	Comments/Action required
The group has agreed terms of reference.	Review programme planning documents	2		

This column requires an assessment to be made, using a 5-point scale, on the extent to which *each* criterion has been achieved. The code for assessing level of achievement is as follows:

1 = Fully achieved
2 = Substantial progress
3 = Partly achieved
4 = Work has commenced
5 = No progress.

Any discrepancy in assigning achievement levels by different assessors will then enable an informed debate to be pursued.

[7.] Completion date

[4] Criteria (Example)	[5] Assessment method	[6] Level of achievement 1–5	[7] Completion date	[8] Comments/Action required
The group has agreed terms of reference.	Review programme planning documents	2	1.12.94	

This requires the date of the full achievement of the criterion to be inserted, either retrospectively or as a forward projection. Non-completion will enable the criterion to be considered in the annual review process and when planning future programmes of work.

[8.] Comments/action required

[4] Criteria (Example)	[5] Assessment method	[6] Level of achievement 1–5	[7] Completion date	[8] Comments/Action required
The group has agreed terms of reference.	Review programme planning documents	2	31.12.94	A first draft has now been agreed. To be confirmed at the next meeting.

This column enables comments to be made concerning the achievement or non-completion of the criterion. It also permits action to be identified (together with those responsible) which will lead to further progress being made. Action to be taken as a result of the assessment is recorded on the summary sheet and can be used to inform future plans.

The summary sheet

At the end of each set of standards is a summary sheet to assist practitioners in summarising performance in respect of each key function. This will enable subjective, as well as objective self-appraisal to be undertaken, encourage a focus upon strengths rather than weaknesses and contribute to the identification of future action plans. It asks the following questions about overall performance on the function:

1. What are your feelings in general about your performance with regard to this function?

2. What, would you say, are your strengths with regard to this function?

3. What scope do you see for further development in this particular area of work?

4. Can you identify priority areas for action with regard to this function?

Standards

The following standards have been developed in consultation with practitioners for the six key functions described. They are offered as a model for you to use or adapt as is appropriate for your circumstances.

1. Strategic planning

Standards

1.1 There is a group which addresses strategic planning issues in health promotion.

1.2 The health promotion service makes an important contribution to the strategic planning group.

1.3 A health promotion strategy is produced and/or health promotion figures prominently within other health strategy documents.

1.4 The health promotion department's plan relates to the health strategies.

2. Programme management

Standards

2.1 A group exists for the planning, implementation and review of each programme area.

2.2 A range of health promotion methods and activities is considered for each programme area in order to determine action plans.

2.3 For each programme area a health promotion specialist is identified who is competent to lead.

2.4 Arrangements are made for reporting on progress.

3. Monitoring and evaluation

Standards

3.1 There are agreed arrangements for monitoring and evaluation of all programmes.

3.2 The results of programme evaluation are used to inform further work.

3.3 Support is given to members of staff to develop their skills with regard to monitoring and/or evaluation.

4. Education and training

Standards

4.1 An education and training plan exists for the health promotion department.

4.2 Training programmes are based upon the results of needs assessment with client groups.

4.3 All training includes an evaluation exercise.

4.4 Training is provided by qualified and experienced trainers.

4.5 Administrative procedures ensure that the training programme is delivered efficiently.

5. Resources and information

Standards

5.1 The provider has a resources and information plan as part of its health promotion strategy or business plan.

5.2 There is a procedure for reviewing the resources and information held in the department.

5.3 The services available are widely advertised for optimal uptake by existing and potential clients.

5.4 Clients feel valued and welcome when visiting the department.

5.5 Resources and information services are adequately housed.

5.6 Clients' views of services are regularly sought and acted upon.

6. Advice and consultancy

Standards

6.1 Staff function within the SHEPS Principles of Practice and Code of Conduct (or equivalent code)

6.2 Advice given is based upon the elicited and expressed needs of clients.

6.3 Confidentiality is maintained at all times with regard to personal information about clients.

6.4 Staff are competent in those aspects of health promotion in which advice is given.

6.5 All staff with an advisory role receive training in communication skills.

Key points

1. Discuss your plans for quality assurance with your staff.

2. Accept that you cannot do everything at once. Introduce your programme gradually and with sensitivity.

3. Make arrangements for someone to have overall responsibility for co-ordinating and managing the programme.

4. Decide on the key areas to use for your quality assurance programme and develop appropriate standards and criteria.

5. The standards and criteria illustrated relate to the six key functions areas chosen to describe health promotion activity.

6. The assessment protocol provides a system for checking performance against these criteria, and enables development of future action plans.

Case study

Health promotion quality standards

Redbridge and Waltham Forest Health Promotion Unit has developed quality standards for training, office procedures and the resources service.

The quality standards on training are based upon quality statements that consider access, equality, approach and delivery. Those on office procedures and resources focus on courtesy, assistance, reliability and efficiency. The Training Programme Co-ordinator has responsibility for ensuring the quality of the training programme. A recent audit of training highlighted the need to consider quality standards relating to trainers in order to ensure the quality of the delivery and content of training. Information about ethnic origin, disability and employment is also routinely collected in line with the Health Promotion Unit's Equal Opportunity Policy.

For further information contact: Mark Thomas or Ann Molyneux, Health Promotion Unit, Thorpe Coombe Hospital, 714 Forest Road, London E17 3HP. Tel: 081-535 6752.

Case study

Salisbury health promotion training scheme quality assurance guidelines

In 1992 Salisbury Health Promotion Unit launched its first year-long training programme. Like many units training had been a core activity but it was decided to establish a more co-ordinated approach. The programme was headed by a co-ordinator and involved all members of the team. In discussing the purpose of the scheme the idea evolved to develop written criteria about how the scheme should be organised. It was then agreed to take this one step further and consider how the team could measure the quality of the training.

Five key areas were identified for assessment:

- use of appropriate facilitators

- safe and appropriate environment

- appropriate evaluation and monitoring

- appropriate resources

- efficient administration.

Through team meetings a set of quality assurance guidelines was formulated and a checklist for trainers devised. For every training course a checklist is completed and given to the co-ordinator for monitoring. The use of the guidelines is regularly reviewed at team meetings.

The main benefits of introducing the guidelines have been identified as greater efficiency in monitoring training and the structure it offers trainers to reflect on and maintain high standards. It also increases trainers' confidence through the positive feedback they receive. The monitoring forms also provide readily accessible information for annual reports and purchasers.

Several gaps in the guidelines have been identified. There are currently no criteria for joining the scheme as a new recruit to the department. There are also no criteria for de-briefing. The guidelines focus more on the process of training than on the content. However, the scheme is still developing and these issues will be addressed through a continuing process of review.

The scheme has been successful for a number of reasons. There was commitment from all involved and the guidelines were devised through consensus. A co-ordinator was appointed to oversee the scheme and meetings were kept to a minimum. The guidelines were presented as a working document which trainers could use but which could also be changed through ongoing review.

For further details contact: Louise Finnis, Senior Health Promotion Officer, Health Promotion Centre, Fonthill, 53 Wilton Road, Salisbury SP2 7EP. Tel 0722 336262, ext. 3061.

5 PURCHASING FOR QUALITY

'Quality assurance will not take root unless it fits the provider culture.'

Summary

This chapter is intended to assist those working in purchasing organisations to purchase quality more effectively in health promotion services. After reading this chapter purchasers should be able to:

1. Identify the role of the purchaser in developing quality assurance in provider organisations.

2. Develop a strategic approach to quality assurance in provider health promotion services.

There are a number of potential problems for purchasers in trying to contract for quality in specialist health promotion services. Purchasing organisations are very new and often work in a process of continuous change. There have been a number of DHA mergers and increasingly there are new joint DHA/FHSA commissioning agencies. Health promotion specialists within purchasing organisations are finding their roles dramatically changing and not all purchasers have such specialists. In some areas the purchaser/provider split is still fluid, with health promotion specialist services still located within the commissioning organisation.

Contracts and service specifications for health promotion are often lacking in detail; there is little consensus on appropriate process or outcome measures for health promotion. Purchasers in general suffer from a lack of good information systems, and information on health promotion is no exception. However, as Duncan Nichol stated in June 1993, 'Every aspect of the NHS has a quality dimension and purchasers need to be focussed and disciplined in their efforts to secure improved quality from providers' (NHSME, 1993b).

An integrated approach

Quality assurance has been defined as planned organisational change (Ellis and Whittington, 1993). It may be useful to use this definition to plan a purchasing strategy for quality health promotion. As a purchaser you may wish to identify your objectives for change in a health promotion provider. Clearly, this process must be approached with sensitivity as the organisation of a health promotion service is a provider rather than a purchaser responsibility. But quality is an appropriate purchaser concern, and thus you may rightly take a strategic view on appropriate methods and potential obstacles to the development of quality assurance. A key element of any such strategy must be to facilitate the creation of a culture of quality within the provider. Quality assurance will not take root unless it fits the provider culture. It is also crucial that your input into provider quality assurance is integrated both with wider purchaser strategy and with the management systems and business planning of providers.

Quality assurance cannot work if it is seen as external to an organisation – if, as we have stressed earlier, no one feels 'ownership' of the process. You must begin by talking to provider managers about the wider quality context in their organisations. Quality activities need to be phased. They need to feed into overall provider systems of organisational review and development. Begin by focusing on those areas where you believe the biggest improvements can be made at the least cost to the provider in terms of time, resources and organisational change. Facilitate change by offering support and models of good practice without being prescriptive about processes which are clearly provider responsibilities. Good communication, dialogue and a sense of common goals are keys to making this work. The focus strategies of education, facilitation, persuasion and power, described by Zaltman and Duncan (Ellis and Whittington, 1993), to manage the development of quality, may provide a useful model for health promotion purchasers to consider (Figure 5.1).

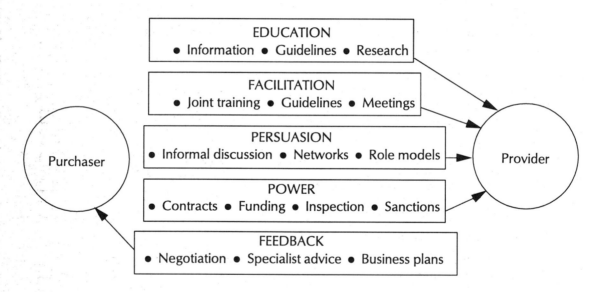

Fig. 5.1. Purchasing strategies for quality assurance in health promotion

SOURCE: Ellis and Whittington, 1993

Contracting for change

Though much of the strategic approach will involve strategies of education, persuasion and facilitation, inevitably some purchasers will also feel the need to use their purchasing power to demand certain standards and monitoring information. Health promotion cannot and should not be insulated from purchasers' responsibilities to contract for change. Before negotiating with providers you may wish to consider what your 'bottom line' is in terms of the standards you wish them to adopt, and the monitoring and feedback mechanisms (Exercise 5.1).

Exercise 5.1

What minimum standards do you wish to see in contracts?

Look at the examples of standards listed below (the full versions are given in Chapter 4) and tick at least five that you would wish to see as minimum standards in contracts.

Strategic planning
There is a group which addresses strategic planning issues in health promotion. ☐

The health promotion service makes an important contribution to the strategic planning group. ☐

Programme management
For each programme area a health promotion specialist is identified who is competent to lead. ☐

A range of health promotion methods and activities is considered for each programme area in order to determine action plans. ☐

Monitoring and evaluation
There are agreed arrangements for monitoring and evaluation of all programmes. ☐

The results of programme evaluation are used to inform further work. ☐

Education and training
An education and training plan exists for the health promotion department. ☐

All training includes an evaluation exercise. ☐

Training is provided by qualified and experienced trainers. ☐

Resources and information
The provider has a resources and information plan as part of its health promotion strategy or business plan. ☐

Clients feel valued and welcome when visiting the department. ☐

Clients' views of services are regularly sought and acted upon. ☐

Advice and consultancy
Staff function within the SHEPS Principles of Practice and Code of Conduct (or equivalent code). ☐

Staff are competent in those aspects of health promotion in which advice is given. ☐

All staff with an advisory role receive training in communication skills. ☐

What other minimum standards would you want to add?

....

We have emphasised in this document how important it is for purchasers and providers to discuss and agree upon the quality of health promotion required. The following case study, though taken from the field of secondary care, offers a model for bringing purchasers and providers together for this purpose.

Case study

Improving communication between purchasers and providers on quality issues

Newcastle General Hospital runs monthly quality days to enable its purchasers to monitor the quality aspects of contracting. It hosts the visits by purchaser quality representatives to the specialty management team of clinical directors, general managers, clinical nurse managers, and the director of nursing and patient care.

Each specialty is visited in turn and presentations are given on: medical audit results; patient satisfaction surveys; nursing audit of patient care; complaints; accidents and incidents; outpatient department waiting times; waiting list admission reports; and specialty-specific quality initiatives.

Twice-yearly meetings are also held on quality initiatives in support areas such as catering, domestic, portering and engineering.

The quality monitoring days are a forum for the provider and purchasers to discuss results openly, share ideas, identify needs and address problems and have provided two-way benefits.

The hospital has benefited from the opportunity to exchange information and to learn from the experience of purchasers who visit other provider units.

For further details contact: Margaret Best, Director of Nursing and Patient Care, Newcastle General Hospital, Newcastle upon Tyne NE4 6BE. Tel: 091 273 8811, ext. 22771.

Purchasing for quality checklist

The Department of Health has recently identified 'hallmarks of effective purchasing' (NHSME, 1993b). These can be used to develop a checklist for effective purchasing of quality health promotion:

- *A strategic approach – i.e. a clear long-term view*
  Have you explicitly identified and documented your strategic approach to developing quality assurance in health promotion through the contracting process?

- *Decision making based on sound intelligence*
  Do you have regular and usable information on health promotion activity levels, costs, achievements, standards and monitoring and evaluation results?

- *Responsiveness to local people*
  Do you have information on the relationship between the health promotion service and local communities? Do you know the degree to which the service involves local people in needs assessment, programme evaluation and quality assurance?

- *External alliances – with GPs and other agencies*
  Have you involved GPs, other agencies and local people in your decisions about purchasing health promotion services, in developing service specifications and in monitoring service delivery?

- *Close working with providers*
  Do you have a close and open relationship with providers of specialist health promotion services and other health promoters?

- *Contracting for quality and value for money*
  Do your service specifications for health promotion include specific quality standards which are measurable, and for which monitoring arrangements have been agreed? Do your service specifications consider cost effectiveness?

- *Organisational fitness to purchase – the maturity of the organisation*
  This chapter has focused on the purchasing of quality from health promotion providers. It is beyond the scope of this pack to address the question of the organisational quality of purchasing agencies. Nevertheless, this is an important issue to which you may wish to give some thought. Your decisions can have a profound impact on providers' ability to deliver a quality health promotion service. The consistency of your purchasing plans, the adequacy of the resources you offer, the realism of your expectations and a range of other purchasing decisions will be key influences on provider quality. Questions you may wish to ask yourself include:

  Is your own organisation a 'quality' purchaser?
  Do you have a quality assurance system in place?
  Is your organisation giving the quality of its purchasing real consideration?

If the answer to any or all of these questions is no, you may wish to consider how you might begin to address quality assurance in purchasing health promotion.

Though much of this document has focused upon the delivery of high quality health promotion there is little doubt that purchasers have a vital role in facilitating such a 'product.' This may be achieved in many ways including, as shown in the following case study, the application of leadership and commitment to quality assurance.

Case study

Purchasing for quality

North West Hertfordshire Purchasing Authority introduced a total quality management (TQM) programme in 1992 to improve the way it works both internally and externally with its providers.

As a first step, a quality audit was conducted which showed that, while the authority worked effectively, quality was seen as something separate and primarily for providers.

Managers attended a two-day workshop to equip them with the skills and knowledge to lead the initiative, and have continuing training sessions.

The TQM initiative is implemented through a quality co-ordinator, a quality council comprising senior managers, and a team of external management consultants. A TQM newsletter is sent to all staff each month. There is also a quality noticeboard in the main corridor.

Early in the process, three audit teams were set up to identify potential areas for improving quality. The teams studied supplier quality assurance, ownership and management, communications, and customers. The teams collected data from inside and outside the organisation using tools such as questionnaires, interviews, and examination of existing records. The teams presented their findings and recommendations to the quality council and members of the purchasing authority. Formal team briefings have been established and this has led to a marked improvement in communication.

An evaluation of activity within departments is in continuous operation. More formalised agreements between internal customers and internal suppliers have led to a stronger working relationship between departments.

One of the most important products that emerged from the initiative was a supplier quality assurance booklet which details explicit standards that the purchaser requires from its providers. Through the use of this document, providers will learn the quality process they must undertake to meet these requirements. This will benefit the end-user by improving services.

The total quality process is being carried forward with teams identifying the cost of quality in terms of failure and prevention and recommending action plans to the quality council.

The process may be represented as follows:

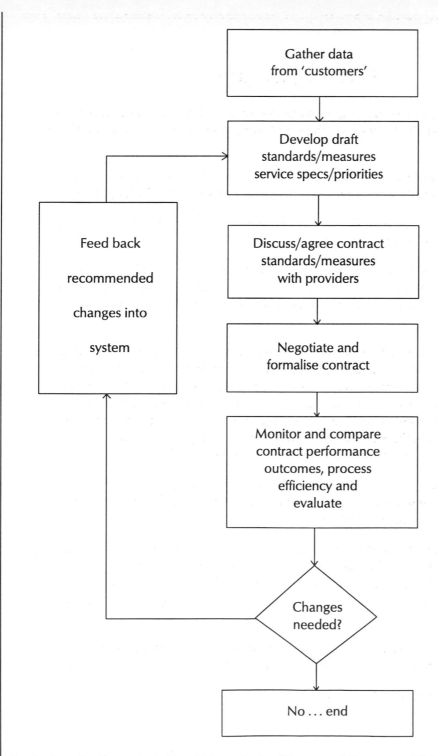

For further details contact: Kate Phipps, Acting Director of Corporate Affairs, North West Hertfordshire Health Authority, St Albans, AL3 5TL. Tel: 0727 866122.

Key points

1. Purchasers need to have a long-term strategic approach to purchasing quality in health promotion.

2. Purchasers may need to use aspects of education, persuasion, facilitation and power strategies to manage the development of quality in health promotion providers.

3. Purchasers should seek to develop a culture of quality within providers.

4. Purchasers will need to understand and work with the diverse organisational structures of providers.

5. Purchasers must identify their quality assurance priorities and minimum standards required as a basis for negotiating quality standards with providers.

6. Purchasers should consider the implications of the 'hallmarks of effective purchasing' for purchasing quality health promotion.

REFERENCES

British Standards Institution (1978) BS 4778: *British Standards Quality Vocabulary.*

Bunton, R. and Macdonald, G. (1992) *Health Promotion: Disciplines and Diversity.* Routledge.

Catford, J. (1993) 'Auditing health promotion: what are the vital signs of quality?' *Health Promotion International* **8**(2): 67–8.

Department of Health (1989) *Working for Patients: the Health Service: Caring for the 1990s,* Cm 555. HMSO.

Department of Health (1992) *The Health of the Nation: a Strategy for Health in England,* Cm 1986. HMSO.

Ellis, R. and Whittingon, D. (1993) *Quality Assurance in Health Care: a Handbook.* Edward Arnold.

Ewles, L. and Simnett, I. (1992) *Promoting Health: a Practical Guide.* Scutari Press, 2nd edn.

Green, L. and Lewis, F. (1986) *Measurement and Evaluation in Health Education and Health Promotion.* Mayfield, Palo Alto, California.

Maxwell, R. (1984) 'Quality assurance in health care', *British Medical Journal,* **288**: 1470–2.

Macdonald, G. (ed.) (1992) *Quality in Health Promotion: Report of the Annual Partnership Conference.* Health Promotion Authority for Wales, Cardiff.

NHS Management Executive (1992) *The Quality Journey: a Guide to Total Quality Management in the NHS.*

NHS Management Executive (1993a) EL(93)54: *Priorities in Planning Guidance 1994/95.*

NHS Management Executive (1993b) *Purchasing for Health: a Framework for Action.* HMSO.

Saan, H. (1993) Personal communication. Dutch Centre for Health Promotion and Health Education.

Society of Health Education and Health Promotion Specialists (1992) *Developing Quality in Health Education and Health Promotion.*

World Health Organization (1984) *Health Promotion: a WHO Document on the Concepts and Principles.*

World Health Organization (1986) *The Ottawa Charter, Principles for Health Promotion.* WHO Regional Office for Europe, Copenhagen.

Wright, C. and Whittington, D. (1992) *Quality Assurance: an Introduction for Health Care Professionals.* Churchill Livingstone.

Appendices

Appendix A   Standards and criteria

1. Strategic planning

Standards

1.1 There is a group which addresses strategic planning issues in health promotion.

1.2 The health promotion service makes an important contribution to the strategic planning group.

1.3 A health promotion strategy is produced and/or health promotion figures prominently within other health strategy documents.

1.4 The health promotion department's plan relates to the health strategies.

Function 1.   Strategic planning

Standard 1.1   There is a group which addresses strategic planning issues in health promotion

Assessor ....   Date of assessment ....

Criteria	Assessment method	Level of achievement 1–5	Date achieved	Comments/Action required
1.1.1 The group has representation from various agencies including: • NHS purchasers and providers • Local authorities • LEA • Voluntary organisations • Community groups. 1.1.2 The group has agreed terms of reference. 1.1.3 Action plans to address health issues exist for each strategy. These specify objectives, targets, resources, timescales, and individual agency responsibilities.				

Level of achievement code: 1 = Fully achieved   2 = Substantial progress   3 = Partly achieved   4 = Work has commenced   5 = No progress

Function 1.   Strategic planning

Standard 1.2   The health promotion service makes an important contribution to the strategic planning group

Assessor...   Date of assessment.................................

Criteria	Assessment method	Level of achievement 1-5	Date achieved	Comments/Action required
1.2.1 A health promotion specialist represents the health promotion service on the strategic group.				
1.2.2 The health promotion service contributes to the development of strategies and action plans.				
1.2.3 The representative feeds back progress to colleagues after each meeting of the multi-agency group.				
1.2.4 The health promotion service reviews its contribution to the strategy planning group annually.				

Level of achievement code: 1 = Fully achieved   2 = Substantial progress   3 = Partly achieved   4 = Work has commenced   5 = No progress

Function 1.   Strategic planning

Standard 1.3   A health promotion strategy is produced and/or health promotion figures prominently within other health strategy documents

Assessor ....   Date of assessment ....

Criteria	Assessment method	Level of achievement 1–5	Date achieved	Comments/Action required
1.3.1 A health promotion strategy exists, or the health promotion components of health strategies produced by the strategic planning group are clearly stated.				
1.3.2 The consultation process for the strategies includes those agencies represented on the strategy group and the wider community.				
1.3.3 The strategy is formally presented to, and accepted by, the health authority/commission and other key agencies.				
1.3.4 Strategies are widely disseminated.				
1.3.5 There are arrangements for annual review of strategies.				

Level of achievement code: 1 = Fully achieved   2 = Substantial progress   3 = Partly achieved   4 = Work has commenced   5 = No progress

Function 1.   Strategic planning

Standard 1.4   The health promotion department's plan relates to the health strategies

Assessor.................................   Date of assessment.................................

Criteria	Assessment method	Level of achievement 1–5	Date achieved	Comments/Action required
1.4.1 A plan for the health promotion service exists based upon the key priority areas for health promotion identified in the health strategies.				
1.4.2 The health promotion service plan reflects the vision, principles and direction outlined in the strategic plan.				
1.4.3 The plan identifies the resources and skills required by the health promotion service to make its full contribution to the strategy.				
1.4.4 The plan identifies the contribution expected of other agencies in support of the implementation of the strategy.				
1.4.5 The plan describes how clients will be involved in decision-making regarding service provision and development.				

Level of achievement code: 1 = Fully achieved   2 = Substantial progress   3 = Partly achieved   4 = Work has commenced   5 = No progress

Summary

Function   Strategic planning

1. What are your feelings in general about your performance with regard to this function?

2. What, would you say, are your strengths with regard to this function?

3. What scope do you see for further development in this particular area of work?

4. Can you identify priority areas for action with regard to this function?

2. Programme management

Standards

2.1 A group exists for the planning, implementation, and review of each programme area.

2.2 A range of health promotion methods and activities is considered for each programme area in order to determine action plans.

2.3 A health promotion specialist who is competent to lead is identified for each programme area.

2.4 Arrangements are made for reporting on progress.

Function 2.   Programme management

Standard 2.1   A group exists for the planning, implementation, and review of each programme area

Assessor ....   Date of assessment ....

Criteria	Assessment method	Level of achievement 1–5	Date achieved	Comments/Action required
2.1.1 A group exists to plan and implement action in each programme area.				
2.1.2 The membership of the group reflects the determinants of the health issue being addressed.				
2.1.3 Terms of reference are formally approved by the group.				
2.1.4 The group has access to appropriate funding.				

Level of achievement code: 1 = Fully achieved   2 = Substantial progress   3 = Partly achieved   4 = Work has commenced   5 = No progress

Function 2.　　　　Programme management

Standard 2.2　　　A range of health promotion methods and activities is considered for each programme area in order to determine
　　　　　　　　　action plans

Assessor........................　　　　　　Date of assessment........................

Criteria	Assessment method	Level of achievement 1–5	Date achieved	Comments/Action required
2.2.1 The group should consider a range of actions that encompasses interventions at the individual, community, structural and environmental levels.				
2.2.2 The group should agree actions on the basis of research or current knowledge of the effectiveness of intervention.				
2.2.3 An action plan is agreed including clear objectives and monitoring procedures.				

Level of achievement code: 1 = Fully achieved　　2 = Substantial progress　　3 = Partly achieved　　4 = Work has commenced　　5 = No progress

Function 2.   Programme management

Standard 2.3   A health promotion specialist who is competent to lead is identified for each programme area

Assessor ....   Date of assessment ....

Criteria	Assessment method	Level of achievement 1–5	Date achieved	Comments/Action required
2.3.1 The health promotion specialist plays a lead role in the planning, co-ordination and evaluation of the programme.				
2.3.2 He/she is eligible for registration as a health promotion specialist.				
2.3.3 Professional development needs are considered for him/her as part of job and departmental review.				
2.3.4 Arrangements are made for any such needs to be met.				
2.3.5 The health promotion specialist is part of a health promotion team or network.				

Level of achievement code: 1 = Fully achieved   2 = Substantial progress   3 = Partly achieved   4 = Work has commenced   5 = No progress

Function 2.   Programme management

Standard 2.4   Arrangements are made for reporting on progress

Assessor.................................   Date of assessment.........................

Criteria	Assessment method	Level of achievement 1–5	Date achieved	Comments/Action required
2.4.1 The production of progress reports is included in the action plan.				
2.4.2 Responsibility for producing the reports is delegated to a named person.				
2.4.3 Reports are distributed to: • all organisations represented on the planning group; • other organisations and community groups as appropriate.				

Level of achievement code: 1 = Fully achieved   2 = Substantial progress   3 = Partly achieved   4 = Work has commenced   5 = No progress

71

Summary

Function   Programme management

1. What are your feelings in general about your performance with regard to this function?

2. What, would you say, are your strengths with regard to this function?

3. What scope do you see for further development in this particular area of work?

4. Can you identify priority areas for action with regard to this function?

3. Monitoring and evaluation

Standards

3.1 There are agreed arrangements for monitoring and evaluation of all programmes.

3.2 The results of programme evaluation are used to inform further work.

3.3 Support is given to relevant members of staff to develop their skills with regard to monitoring and/or evaluation.

Function 3   Monitoring and evaluation

Standard 3.1   There are agreed arrangements for monitoring and evaluation of all programmes

Assessor ....   Date of assessment ....

Criteria	Assessment method	Level of achievement 1–5	Date achieved	Comments/Action required
3.1.1 The programme plan clearly identifies how it will be monitored, who is responsible for it, timetable and reporting mechanism.				
3.1.2 An evaluation plan describing methodology is agreed for each major programme area.				
3.1.3 Monitoring and evaluation methods used are valid, reliable and appropriate.				
3.1.4 Resources are allocated to enable implementation of the monitoring and evaluation plans.				

Level of achievement code: 1 = Fully achieved   2 = Substantial progress   3 = Partly achieved   4 = Work has commenced   5 = No progress

Function 3. Monitoring and evaluation

Standard 3.2 The results of programme evaluation are used to inform further work

Assessor................................ Date of assessment................

Criteria	Assessment method	Level of achievement 1–5	Date achieved	Comments/Action required
3.2.1 Regular progress reports are made on all major programmes and widely disseminated.				
3.2.2 Results of routine monitoring and research activities inform future action planning.				

Level of achievement code: 1 = Fully achieved   2 = Substantial progress   3 = Partly achieved   4 = Work has commenced   5 = No progress

Function 3. Monitoring and evaluation

Standard 3.3 Support is given to relevant members of staff to develop their skills with regard to monitoring and/or evaluation .

Assessor .... Date of assessment ....

Criteria	Assessment method	Level of achievement 1–5	Date achieved	Comments/Action required
3.3.1 Staff are given the opportunity to identify personal training needs with regard to monitoring and/or evaluation.				
3.3.2 Arrangements are made for staff to receive appropriate training in order to meet their identified needs.				
3.3.3 Plans exist for reviewing the need for any further training with regard to monitoring and/or evaluation.				

Level of achievement code: 1 = Fully achieved   2 = Substantial progress   3 = Partly achieved   4 = Work has commenced   5 = No progress

Summary

Function   Monitoring and evaluation

1. What are your feelings in general about your performance with regard to this function?

2. What, would you say, are your strengths with regard to this function?

3. What scope do you see for further development in this particular area of work?

4. Can you identify priority areas for action with regard to this function?

4. Education and training

Standards

4.1 An education and training plan exists for the health promotion department.

4.2 Training programmes are based upon the results of needs assessment with client groups.

4.3 All training includes an evaluation exercise.

4.4 Training is provided by qualified and experienced trainers.

4.5 Administrative procedures ensure that the training programme is delivered efficiently.

Function 4.   Education and training

Standard 4.1   An education and training plan exists for the health promotion department

Assessor..   Date of assessment.........................

Criteria	Assessment method	Level of achievement 1–5	Date achieved	Comments/Action required
4.1.1 Consultation has been carried out with other people with a training responsibility both within and outside the NHS.				
4.1.2 A senior member of staff is delegated with a departmental responsibility for co-ordination of education and training.				
4.1.3 The department produces a training programme based upon the plan, and publicises it widely.				

Level of achievement code: 1 = Fully achieved   2 = Substantial progress   3 = Partly achieved   4 = Work has commenced   5 = No progress

Function 4.   Education and training

Standard 4.2   Training programmes are based upon the results of needs assessment with client groups

Assessor ....   Date of assessment ....

Criteria	Assessment method	Level of achievement 1–5	Date achieved	Comments/Action required
4.2.1 A process for undertaking a regular needs assessment with client groups is agreed.				
4.2.2 Agencies in the NHS, local authorities, the private and voluntary sectors are approached to assess their training needs.				
4.2.3 The training programme reflects the needs identified.				

Level of achievement code: 1 = Fully achieved   2 = Substantial progress   3 = Partly achieved   4 = Work has commenced   5 = No progress

Function 4.   Education and training

Standard 4.3   All training includes an evaluation exercise

Assessor..   Date of assessment..

Criteria	Assessment method	Level of achievement 1–5	Date achieved	Comments/Action required
4.3.1 All training currently provided includes an evaluation exercise upon completion.				
4.3.2 A follow-up evaluation after 3–6 months is undertaken on a sample of courses/trainees to assess the extent to which the training *is being implemented*.				
4.3.3 The outcome of the evaluation is used to inform the provision of training in the future.				

Level of achievement code: 1 = Fully achieved   2 = Substantial progress   3 = Partly achieved   4 = Work has commenced   5 = No progress

Function 4.   Education and training

Standard 4.4   Training is provided by qualified and experienced trainers

Assessor ....   Date of assessment ....

Criteria	Assessment method	Level of achievement 1–5	Date achieved	Comments/Action required
4.4.1 The education and training plan identifies eligibility to contribute to the health promotion department's training programme.				
4.4.2 Arrangements exist for approving those contributing to the departmental training programme. This is reviewed annually.				
4.4.3 A mechanism exists for planning the content and ensuring continuity between those contributing to the training programme.				
4.4.4 Trainers are required to demonstrate, or have certification in, presentation skills in addition to expertise in content area.				

Standard 4.4 continued

Criteria	Assessment method	Level of achievement 1-5	Date achieved	Comments/Action required
4.4.5 Trainers have, or are given, an understanding of health promotion theory and practice before being accepted into the programme.				
4.4.6 Trainers have to accept the SHEPS Principles of Practice and Code of Conduct as a condition of becoming an 'approved' trainer.				
4.4.7 A procedure is agreed for debriefing with co-trainers to consider evaluation.				

Level of achievement code: 1 = Fully achieved   2 = Substantial progress   3 = Partly achieved   4 = Work has commenced   5 = No progress

Function 4.   Education and training

Standard 4.5   Administrative procedures ensure that the training programme is delivered efficiently

Assessor ....   Date of assessment ....

Criteria	Assessment method	Level of achievement 1–5	Date achieved	Comments/Action required
4.5.1 Guidelines are provided for trainers with regard to standards and procedures.				
4.5.2 There are agreed administrative procedures for publicity; notification and confirmation of places; and directions.				
4.5.3 Venues provide an appropriate environment, including disabled access and compliance with Health and Safety legislation.				

Level of achievement code: 1 = Fully achieved   2 = Substantial progress   3 = Partly achieved   4 = Work has commenced   5 = No progress

Summary

Function   Education and training

1. What are your feelings in general about your performance with regard to this function?

2. What, would you say, are your strengths with regard to this function?

3. What scope do you see for further development in this particular area of work?

4. Can you identify priority areas for action with regard to this function?

5. Resources and information

Standards

5.1 The provider has a resources and information plan as part of its health promotion strategy or business plan.

5.2 There is a procedure for reviewing the resources and information held in the department.

5.3 The services available are widely advertised for optimal uptake by existing and potential clients.

5.4 Clients feel valued and welcome when visiting the department.

5.5 Resources and information services are adequately housed.

5.6 Clients' views of services are regularly sought and acted upon.

Function 5.   Resources and information

Standard 5.1   The provider has a resources and information plan as part of its health promotion strategy or business plan

Assessor.................................   Date of assessment.................................

Criteria	Assessment method	Level of achievement 1–5	Date achieved	Comments/Action required
5.1.1 The plan is clearly identified within the health promotion strategy or business plan.				
5.1.2 The plan is brought to the attention of clients.				
5.1.3 A senior member of staff is designated with responsibility for implementing the plan.				
5.1.4 There is an agreed review process for the plan.				

Level of achievement code: 1 = Fully achieved   2 = Substantial progress   3 = Partly achieved   4 = Work has commenced   5 = No progress

Function 5.   Resources and information

Standard 5.2   There is a procedure for reviewing the resources and information held in the department

Assessor ....   Date of assessment ....

Criteria	Assessment method	Level of achievement 1–5	Date achieved	Comments/Action required
5.2.1 A statement is agreed for ensuring that resources are accurate, non-prejudicial and appropriate to the needs of clients.				
5.2.2 There is an agreed procedure for reviewing materials, which involves health promotion specialists.				
5.2.3 Arrangements exist for previewing and evaluating new resources.				
5.2.4 Advice is sought from other health professionals with regard to new resources in their field of work.				

Level of achievement code: 1 = Fully achieved   2 = Substantial progress   3 = Partly achieved   4 = Work has commenced   5 = No progress

Function 5.   Resources and information

Standard 5.3   The services available are widely advertised for optimal uptake by existing and potential clients

Assessor.....................   Date of assessment...................

Criteria	Assessment method	Level of achievement 1–5	Date achieved	Comments/Action required
5.3.1 A member of staff is delegated with responsibility for promoting the services.				
5.3.2 There is a planned programme to publicise the services provided.				
5.3.3 Efforts are continually being made to attract new clients.				
5.3.4 Records are maintained on the use of resources and information by client groups.				
5.3.5 Quarterly reports are made on the uptake of resources and information support services.				

Level of achievement code: 1 = Fully achieved   2 = Substantial progress   3 = Partly achieved   4 = Work has commenced   5 = No progress

89

Function 5.   Resources and information

Standard 5.4   Clients feel valued and welcome when visiting the department

Assessor ....   Date of assessment ....

Criteria	Assessment method	Level of achievement 1–5	Date achieved	Comments/Action required
5.4.1 Direction signs are clearly available for visitors to locate the department.				
5.4.2 The reception or enquiry point is at the entrance to the department.				
5.4.3 The receptionist has undergone training for his/her work.				
5.4.4 An explanation is always given to visitors for any delay in receiving attention.				
5.4.5 Staff identify themselves both verbally and with name badges.				
5.4.6 Staff have received training in telephone and personal communication skills.				

Level of achievement code: 1 = Fully achieved   2 = Substantial progress   3 = Partly achieved   4 = Work has commenced   5 = No progress

Function 5.   Resources and information

Standard 5.5   Resources and information services are adequately housed

Assessor................................   Date of assessment................

Criteria	Assessment method	Level of achievement 1–5	Date achieved	Comments/Action required
5.5.1 There is sufficient parking for visitors to the department.				
5.5.2 There is good access for deliveries to be made to the department.				
5.5.3 Adequate space is provided for the storage and display of resources and information.				
5.5.4 A suitable area is available for clients to wait and then preview materials.				
5.5.5 Adequate help is available to staff with regard to the handling of materials and equipment.				
5.5.6 All staff have undergone training in lifting and handling.				

Level of achievement code: 1 = Fully achieved   2 = Substantial progress   3 = Partly achieved   4 = Work has commenced   5 = No progress

Function 5. Resources and information

Standard 5.6 Clients' views of services are regularly sought and acted upon

Assessor .... Date of assessment ....

Criteria	Assessment method	Level of achievement 1–5	Date achieved	Comments/Action required
5.6.1 A facility exists for clients to express their needs and comment on the service received.				
5.6.2 A report is produced on clients' expressed needs.				
5.6.3 Where appropriate services cannot be provided arrangements exist for referral to other sources of information.				

Level of achievement code: 1 = Fully achieved   2 = Substantial progress   3 = Partly achieved   4 = Work has commenced   5 = No progress

Summary

Function   Resources and information

1. What are your feelings in general about your performance with regard to this function?

2. What, would you say, are your strengths with regard to this function?

3. What scope do you see for further development in this particular area of work?

4. Can you identify priority areas for action with regard to this function?

6. Advice and consultancy

Standards

6.1 Staff function within the SHEPS Principles of Practice and Code of Conduct (or equivalent code).

6.2 Advice given is based upon the elicited and expressed needs of clients.

6.3 Confidentiality is maintained at all times with regard to personal information about clients.

6.4 Staff are competent in those aspects of health promotion in which advice is given.

6.5 All staff with an advisory role receive training in communication skills.

Function 6. Advice and consultancy

Standard 6.1 Staff function within the SHEPS Principles of Practice and Code of Conduct (or equivalent code)

Assessor................................ Date of assessment................................

Criteria	Assessment method	Level of achievement 1–5	Date achieved	Comments/Action required
6.1.1 The SHEPS document (or equivalent) is discussed formally with all staff.				
6.1.2 The document is accepted as a framework or set of guidelines within which to work.				
6.1.3 Arrangements are made for reviewing the contents of the document and its application.				

Level of achievement code: 1 = Fully achieved   2 = Substantial progress   3 = Partly achieved   4 = Work has commenced   5 = No progress

Function 6.   Advice and consultancy

Standard 6.2   Advice given is based upon the elicited and expressed needs of clients

Assessor ....   Date of assessment ....

Criteria	Assessment method	Level of achievement 1–5	Date achieved	Comments/Action required
6.2.1 All staff receive training in how to help clients to identify and express their needs.				
6.2.2. There is a written statement on the department's philosophy and ethical considerations when giving advice to clients.				
6.2.3 Records are kept of the help given to individual clients whilst retaining confidentiality.				

Level of achievement code: 1 = Fully achieved   2 = Substantial progress   3 = Partly achieved   4 = Work has commenced   5 = No progress

Function 6.   Advice and consultancy

Standard 6.3   Confidentiality is maintained at all times with regard to personal information about clients

Assessor............................   Date of assessment............................

Criteria	Assessment method	Level of achievement 1–5	Date achieved	Comments/Action required
6.3.1 All staff comply with the requirements of the Data Protection Act and any other relevant policy of their employer.				
6.3.2 This issue has been discussed formally with staff in the last two years.				
6.3.3 Precautions are taken to safeguard written records of personal information about clients.				
6.3.4 Sanctions exist should confidentiality be seriously, or regularly, breached.				

Level of achievement code: 1 = Fully achieved   2 = Substantial progress   3 = Partly achieved   4 = Work has commenced   5 = No progress

Function 6.　　　Advice and consultancy

Standard 6.4　　　Staff are competent in those aspects of health promotion in which advice is given

Assessor ....　　　Date of assessment ....

Criteria	Assessment method	Level of achievement 1–5	Date achieved	Comments/Action required
6.4.1 Arrangements are made for regular review of the technical competence of staff in their advisory role.				
6.4.2 Staff undertake continuing education and training which will update them in their particular aspect of health promotion.				
6.4.3 A specific budget is allocated for staff training in terms of technical expertise.				

Level of achievement code: 1 = Fully achieved　2 = Substantial progress　3 = Partly achieved　4 = Work has commenced　5 = No progress

Function 6.   Advice and consultancy

Standard 6.5   All staff with an advisory role receive training in communication skills

Assessor..   Date of assessment..

Criteria	Assessment method	Level of achievement 1–5	Date achieved	Comments/Action required
6.5.1 Where staff have an advisory role this is clearly recognised in the job description or staff appraisal system.				
6.5.2 Personal training needs for communication, counselling or any other aspect of the advisory role are identified.				
6.5.3 Staff undertake continuing education in order to meet such needs.				

Level of achievement code: 1 = Fully achieved   2 = Substantial progress   3 = Partly achieved   4 = Work has commenced   5 = No progress

Summary

Function   Advice and consultancy

1. What are your feelings in general about your performance with regard to this function?

2. What, would you say, are your strengths with regard to this function?

3. What scope do you see for further development in this particular area of work?

4. Can you identify priority areas for action with regard to this function?

Appendix B   Summary of the consultation process

Project commenced	January 1993
Discussion with Wessex Health Promotion Managers and Specialists	February to April 1993
Seminar – Wessex Branch of SHEPS	27 April 1993
Further contact with Health Promotion Managers in Wessex	May 1993
Oxford RHA Audit Conference	21 June 1993
HEA Strategic Advisory Group Meeting	29 June 1993
Northern Region Health Promotion Managers' Meeting	14 July 1993
Health Promotion Managers and Consultants' Meeting – Bristol	12 August 1993
Wessex Health Promotion Managers and other specialists – comments on draft document	September 1993
International Summer School Workshop, Cardiff	16 September 1993
Trent Health Promotion Managers' Meeting	17 September 1993
National selection of managers, specialists and academic course tutors – comments on final draft	December 1993
Piloting of quality standards in selected Wessex and South Western health promotion units	December 1993

Appendix C   Project management committee

Patricia Christmas (Chair)

Assistant Director of Public Health (Health Promotion), Southampton and SW Hants Health Commission

David Evans

Research Fellow, Institute for Health Policy Studies, University of Southampton (Formerly Sexual Health and HIV Programme Manager, Salisbury Health Authority)

Professor John Gabbay

Director, Wessex Institute of Public Health Medicine, University of Southampton

Dr Michael Head

Formerly Health Promotion Manager, Dorset Health Commission.
Now a health promotion consultant based at Bournemouth University

Elizabeth Lowe

Quality Development Manager, Wiltshire and Bath Health Commission (Formerly Regional Quality Development Manager, Wessex Regional Health Authority)

Dr Viv Speller (Project Manager)

Director of Health Promotion, Wessex Institute of Public Health Medicine, University of Southampton

Russell Caplan

Project Officer, Health Education Authority

Appendix D Glossary

Accessibility | Describes whether a service is easily available to users in terms of time, distance and ethos.

Acceptability | Describes whether a service or practice satisfies the reasonable expectations of users.

Appropriateness | Describes whether a service or practice is that which the user requires.

Audit | The systematic critical analysis of the quality of a health promotion programme. Considered here to be synonymous with quality assurance. Sometimes used to describe the review stage in a quality assurance process.

Cost benefit analysis | An assessment of the costs and the benefits of a programme in order to determine if one outweighs the other.

Cost-effectiveness | The extent to which a service can achieve its objectives for a minimum cost.

Criteria | Descriptive statements which are measurable, that relate to a standard. Sometimes the term 'indicator' is used synonymously.

Effectiveness | Extent to which a service achieves its intended objectives.

Efficacy | A measure of demonstrable beneficial effect.

Efficiency | Producing maximum benefit with minimum cost.

Equity | Ensuring that users have equal access to and/or equal benefit from services.

Evaluation | The process of collecting and analysing information about the effectiveness of phases of a programme or the programme as a whole. It involves assessing programme achievements. Evaluation may refer to processes and/or outcomes.

Monitoring | The process of collecting and analysing information about programme implementation over time to ensure planned activities are carried out and problems are identified.

Needs assessment | The systematic assessment of a population's needs, balancing epidemiological data, user and public views, provider information, research and other information sources as appropriate.

Outcome evaluation	Analysis of the extent to which a programme achieved its intended objectives.
Quality	A level of excellence identified by an agreed standard. It may be used to mean a level of excellence.
Quality assurance	The systematic process through which achievable and desirable levels of quality are described, the extent to which these levels are achieved is assessed, and action is taken following assessment to enable them to be reached.
Relevance	The degree to which services provided relate to the needs of users.
Research	Describes a spectrum of logical and systematic methods for answering original questions. Research methodologies range from statistical analysis to ethnographic studies.
Responsiveness	The extent to which the service adapts to the expressed needs of users.
Standard	A statement which defines an agreed level of excellence.

Appendix E   Sample standards assessment form and Summary sheet

Function...

Standard...

Assessor.....................................   Date of assessment.........................

Criteria	Assessment method	Level of achievement 1-5	Date achieved	Comments/Action required

Level of achievement code: 1 = Fully achieved   2 = Substantial progress   3 = Partly achieved   4 = Work has commenced   5 = No progress

Summary sheet

Function

1. What are your feelings in general about your performance with regard to this function?

2. What, would you say, are your strengths with regard to this function?

3. What scope do you see for further development in this particular area of work?

4. Can you identify priority areas for action with regard to this function?